A Hundred Years in Wester Ross: 1

Introduction

A Bittersweet Century

This book is about the people and the communities of Wester Ross, and how their way of life evolved and progressed (or not) during the 20th century. The format of the text is to focus on stories which made news in the first year of each decade, with snippets from other years.

Pictures have been chosen to illustrate developments mentioned in the text, so there are few landscapes.

Everyone, of course, has specially important memories of their own to add to the story, but sadly there is not space to include each and every significant event.

Of course, society in all regions of Britain, not just here, changed greatly during the 20th century. But few communities faced challenges as extreme as in Wester Ross and the West Highlands. Here, in the mid-century, there were serious concerns that whole districts would become depopulated. A culture and way of life seemed under threat. Society was still Gaelic in essence - even though the language was no longer much spoken - but too many of the young people were leaving.

New Dawn

It is hard to believe, but no-one is alive now to recall the start of the 20th century on 1st January 1900. We can only imagine how people must have felt. They must surely have longed to believe life would improve, if not for their sake then for their children.

Local people then had little sense of power over their destiny. The mid-19th century had brought great hardship - the clearances, famines, forced emigration - from which the government had failed to offer any protection. It was only recently that legislation had guaranteed even a roof over most heads. The choice of occupations remained limited. Fishing and crofting were still the mainstay of a fragile economy and there was no welfare state to offer support. People had grown resigned to seeing children or grandchildren leave the Highlands in search of better prospects. Despite this, or perhaps because of it, many people had deep religious faith.

Mixed Blessings

What would people of 1900 have felt if foresight had allowed them to see the changes coming? Had they seen no further than 1950, perhaps foreboding. But life in 2000 would have inspired a mixture of emotions.

Astonishment, surely, at the progress in healthcare and housing, and technology in all its forms from hydro-electric power-stations to television and jet aircraft.

Pleasure, no doubt, that many descendants remain and are living well. Pride, that many others went on to achieve success elsewhere in Britain and overseas.

Sadness at the cruel toll of war-time. Sadness also at empty churches and that the Sabbath is so little respected; at the loss of so many old ways, and that Gaelic is so rarely spoken. Perhaps relief, that history now at least acknowledges the truth of the Highland Clearances.

Astonishment that fish are now farmed, and otters and pine-martens 'protected', that there are so many commercial forests and nature reserves; at the amount of red tape in our lives and at the supermarkets that sell products from all over the world including that oddest of products, water.

Sadness at modern problems unknown in 1900: pollution, waste, vandalism. Sadness that, despite the progress made during the century, it came too late to prevent whole communities from disappearing.

The 20th century brought great changes, mostly for the better but some for the worse. It is, in short, a bittersweet tale.

Articles

Map Illustrations

Maps reproduced by kind permission of the Trustees of the National Library of Scotland

Information Sources

Most of the press extracts are from the *Ross-shire Journal*. Other media sources are the *West Highland Free Press* (from 1972), the *Ullapool News* (1973), the *Gairloch and District Times* (1978), *An Carrannach* (1985), and *Wester Ross Life* (1994-98).

Statistics are given for the seven parishes of Glenshiel, Kintail, Lochalsh, Lochcarron, Applecross, Gairloch and Lochbroom. These exclude the inland area of Contin parish west of Garve; but there are references to that area in the text, as also to the county town of Dingwall.

Extracts from several articles in previous issues of *Wester Ross Life* are re-printed, with thanks to their authors.

Published by D.Shaw, 41 Morefield Place, Ullapool IV26 2TS, and printed by Highland Printers, Inverness. Special thanks to the Ross-shire Journal, of which back copies can be consulted at Inverness Reference Library.

It would be a pleasure to hear from readers with reminiscences or photographs which you would be willing to contribute for future publication.

Published for the first time in the UK by D.Shaw
41 Morefield Place, Ullapool IV26 2TS

ISBN 0 9543691 0 6

Printed by Highland Printers

Acknowledgments

A number of contributors provided information, some of whom previously contributed to *Wester Ross Life*, and their goodwill is much appreciated. The maps are from the 1904 Ordnance Survey 1:2500 series (Ross & Cromarty), reproduced by permission of the Trustees of the National Library of Scotland. Photographs by kind permission of Clarrie Pashley; Charlie Allen; Brenda G.Macrow; Mary Hudson *(p.9, top)*; the Campbell family; Marie Wilson; Alex MacRae; Donald MacCormick *(p.30, top)*; Highland Council Museums Service, Portree *(p.9, top,* and *p.13)*; the Royal Commission on the Ancient & Historical Monuments of Scotland *(p.30, centre* and *bottom, p.63, bottom, all Crown Copyright)*; Tain through Time *(p.40, bottom)*; Aberdeen University *(below* and *p.9, bottom* and *p.32, both)*; the National Archives of Scotland *(p.13, bottom - ref. BR/HR/4/27)*; and the Scottish Life Archive of the National Museums of Scotland *(p.18, bottom, p.30, top, p.37, top, p.40, bottom* and *p.63, top)*. Special thanks to Isabel Mackenzie and Willie MacKintosh for their help. Colonel Fairrie, Fort George, kindly provided information about John Mackenzie.

Front cover: Loch Kishorn and oil platform fabrication yard *(C.Pashley)*. *Back cover:* RNLI station, Kyle

Cottages at Ardnarff, Lochcarron, around the turn of the century

George Washington Wilson

Diary of a Year

1900

The Lovat Scouts are Raised

The 20th century began with a remarkable throwback to the era of the late 18th century when lairds like Seaforth had raised regiments for the British Army. This time it was Lord Lovat, whose "patriotic efforts to raise a corps of ghillies to act as scouts in South Africa" were praised by the *Ross-shire Journal* in January. "Men are being steadily enrolled and horses, equipment, and subscriptions in cash are being received." Many men from Wester Ross, where the Frasers of Lovat had at one time owned large areas of land, would later serve with the regiment in the world wars.

Gairloch Men at the Front

It was reported in May that eight men of the Gairloch Volunteer Company had been accepted for service in South Africa. Two had joined the Lovat Scouts, five others the Highland Brigade, and one, Kenneth Mackenzie, the Imperial Yeomanry.

Kenneth's brother James was currently reported to be trapped in Mafeking, which was under siege by the Boers. It was relieved on 17th May, unfortunately too late for James, who died of fever some weeks later.

The *Ross-shire Journal* praised the Gairloch men's willingness to enlist. *A great many more men have volunteered, and it says much for the enthusiam of this company that about 60 members will go under canvas at Fort George for a fortnight towards the end of June.* This reference was to the annual camp of the Highland Volunteer Brigade.

Celebrating the Old New Year

The annual ball for employees of the Highland Railway Company in the Kyle district was held on 13th January - Old New Year's Eve.

The proceedings commenced at Fernbank at 10pm, and were heartily taken part in until midnight, when the company adjourned to the Kyle Hotel, where a hearty repast was served by Mr Urquhart, the proprietor. After supper, dancing was resumed, and kept up with great enthusiasm until 5 o'clock in the morning, when a very enjoyable entertainment was brought to a close by the singing of Auld Lang Syne.

Ross-Shire Journal, 19th January

The re-opening of Poolewe public hall in January after repairs was welcomed, especially as the daily and illustrated papers were on display and these were of great interest with the South African war now going on.

Controversial Church Union

In the autumn of 1900 there was intense discussion in the Highlands about a proposed amalgamation between the Free Church of Scotland and the United Presbyterian Church. The amalgamation went ahead, resulting in the formation of the United Free Church.

But some congregations, mostly in the Highlands, decided not to approve the merger, continuing as the Free Church of Scotland - ever afterwards to be known, in common parlance, as the 'Wee Frees'.

The strength of feeling was such that some ministers who decided to join the United Free Church lost most of their congregations. On the first Sunday after the union was declared, the congregation in Poolewe Church numbered just thirteen, and by the following week had fallen to eight.

"The great bulk of the congregation and their elders held meetings of their own in the school," reported the *Ross-shire Journal*. The paper expressed a sense of shock, for the minister, Mr Dingwall, had been in the parish for many years and had served the community not only as a pastor but as a medic.

New Church at Kyle

Construction of the Church of Scotland at Kyle was begun.

No More Whisky

Revenue men seized a still in Kintail: another battle won (or lost) in the war of wits between them and locals who saw it as their perfect right to make whisky.

Letter from South Africa

This letter was published in the Ross-shire Journal on 5th January 1900. It was written near the front line at Modder River by a corporal in the Seaforth Highlanders.

We have just arrived in this camp today, and it is the first time the brigade has been together since we landed. We are going to advance on Kimberley in a few days, so we expect a big fight before we get there. It is only 18 miles from Modder River camp.

You would not know the regiment now if you saw it, the changes being khaki aprons, no sporrans, stripes, nor ribbons. Everything that would make a mark for the Boers has to be taken off. The troops have all big whiskers, and they look pure warriors.

Officers have to carry rifles, sling and ammunition the same as 'Tommy', in place of their swords and revolvers, and you can have an idea how it doubles them up carrying a blanket on their shoulders and a greatcoat on the waistbelt. The regiment is in excellent health, there being scarcely any sickness. We have about 12,000 infantry in our division here, besides artillery and cavalry. The country up here is similar to that of Egypt, but not so hot, being very sandy. We have intense heat through the day and extreme cold at night. We pass the nights very well with our chums of the Highland Light Infantry, Black Watch and Argylls. The Brigade of Guards is also camped very near to us.

We had a very long voyage of 28 days coming out, and were nearly starved to death. The food is decent enough here, but the water is of a very inferior class. We took 39 dead Boers out of the river who were killed in the battle here a week ago, so you can have an idea what like it was. The troops who were in the engagement are in excellent spirits, and we are all longing to have another bash at the Boers.

On 10th-11th January, British forces suffered heavy losses at Modder River. Readers of the Ross-shire Journal were urged to donate items of clothing for the men at the front: woollen shirts, socks, cholera belts, knitted helmets, sleeping caps. Donations were to be sent to Mrs Mackenzie of Gairloch Estate. In mid-January came news that the siege of Ladysmith had been ended, at a cost of 149 British lives. Ladysmith was again besieged in February.

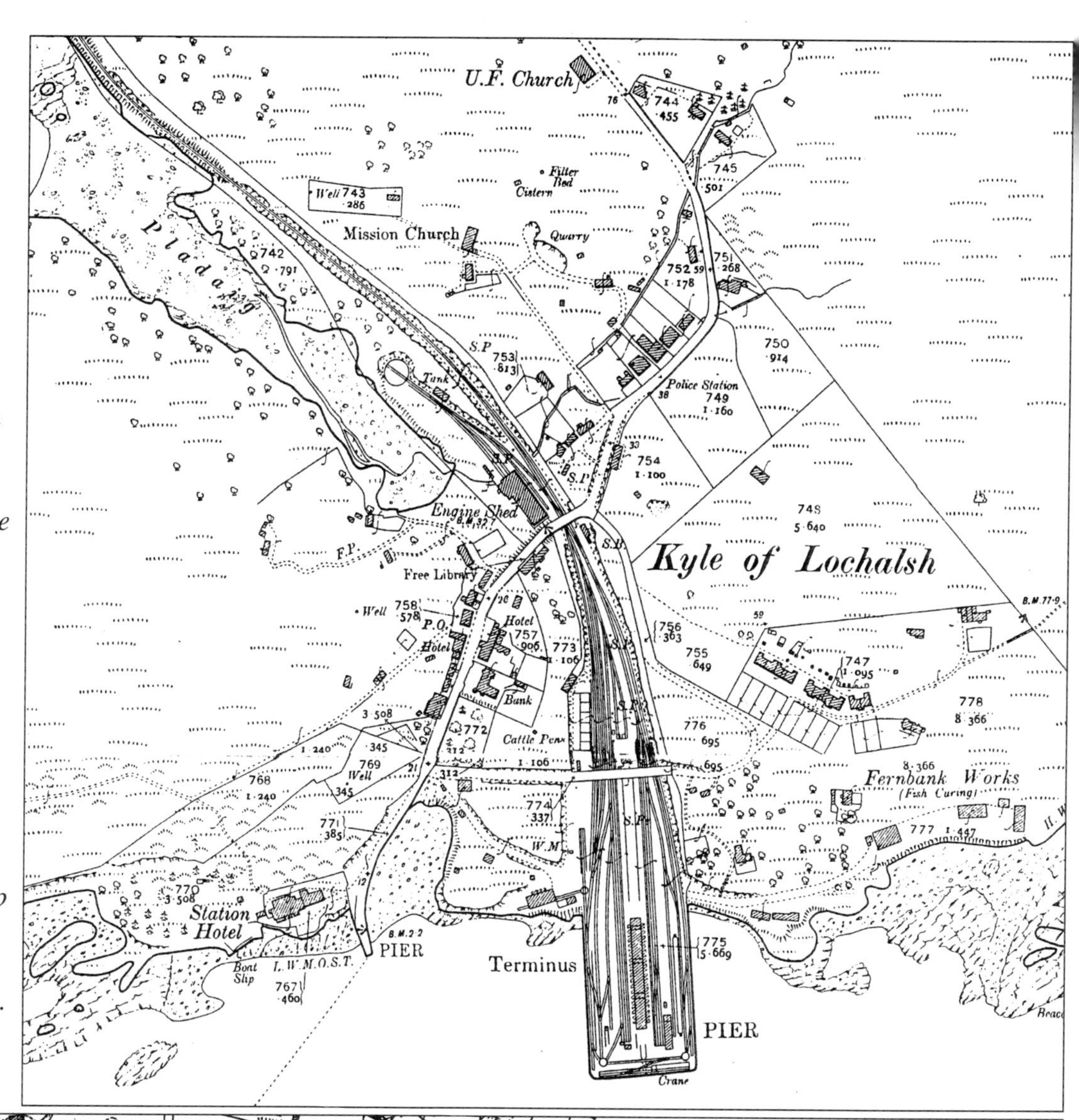

Right: Map of Kyle, 1904.

The road into the village is from the north through Badicaul, not from the east as today (that road opened in 1970). At this time it is just seven years since the railway line extended to Kyle, and railway works still dominate the scene.

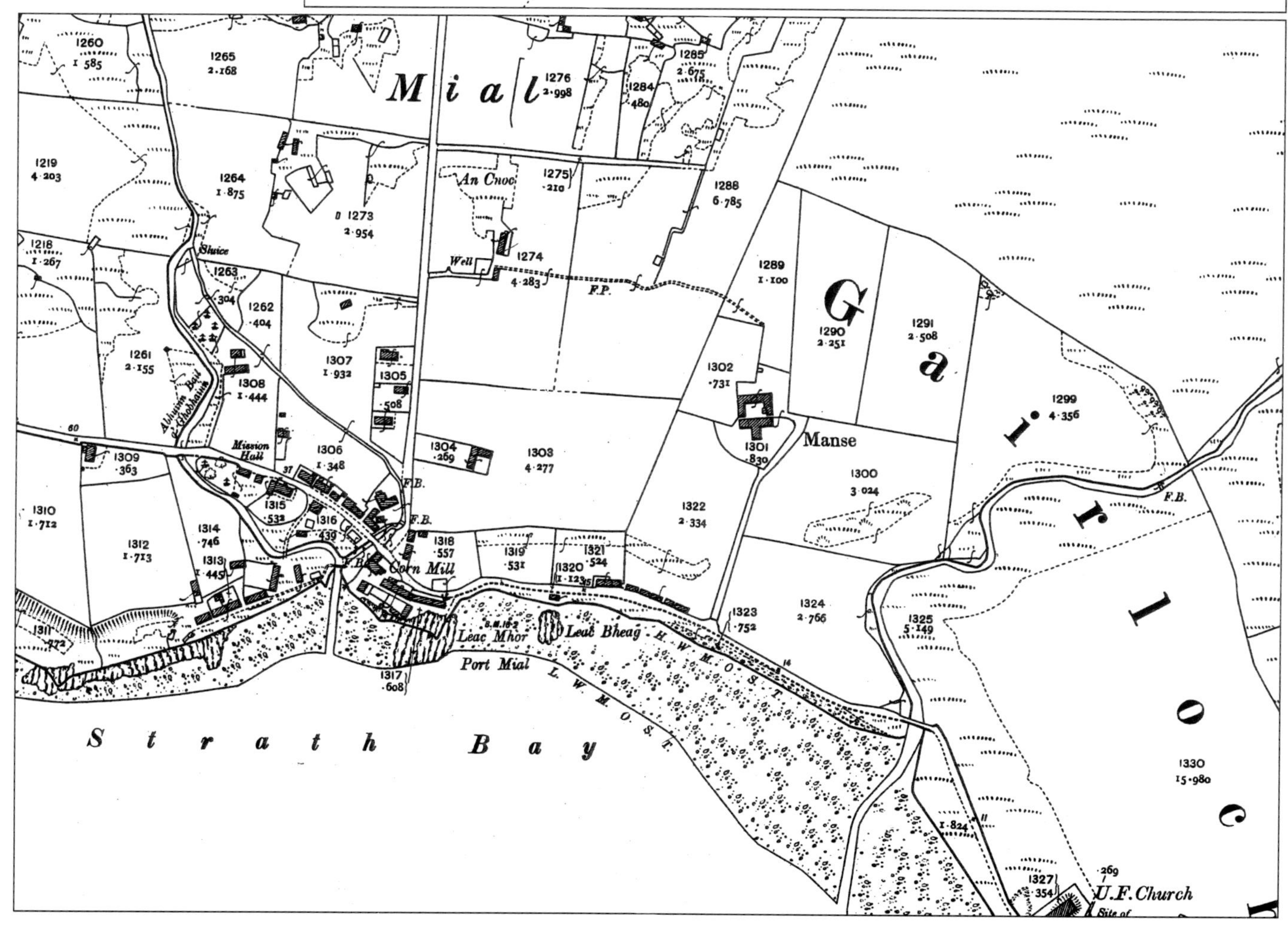

Below: Map of Strath, Gairloch, 1904.

Like other Wester Ross villages, Strath would slowly develop during the century. The mill belonged to Mr Forbes (see p.28).

Lieutenant Alistair Murray, son of the proprietor of Lochcarron Estate, died from wounds received as he advanced against the Boers at Senekal with the Grenadier Guards in June.

Helping the War Effort

People of Applecross sent a parcel of 200 pairs of socks and various other articles

1900 (continued)

to Lady Middleton, to be sent to the troops in South Africa.

Flannan Isles Mystery

As 1900 closed, the disappearance of three lighthouse-keepers from the remote Flannan Isles mystified the nation.

On Holiday

Tourism was in its infancy in 1900. Few people had the money or the time for a holiday, especially in a remote area like Wester Ross.

Accommodation was offered by 22 hotels, with the Gairloch Hotel unusual in its size; most had only a few rooms, with a staff of five or six. The Kyle Hotel had a cook, waitress, housemaid and porter in addition to the hotelkeeper. The temperance ethic was very strong at this time, and Temperance Hotels (dry) were open in Kyle, Applecross and Shieldaig, where Mary-Ann MacLean remained the proprietor until the 1940s.

Letter from South Africa (2)

This is from a letter by a private in the Seaforth Highlanders, in December 1900

We got the order to go to Jagersfontein, as the Boers had risen and were doing some damage to the English.

The Boer commandant got about 500 Boers into the town, into his garden, in the night-time. The Seaforths were lying in the town square, about ten yards from the house, and as the cooks got up in the early morning to make breakfast, and were putting on their kilts, the Boers opened fire on them from behind the wall about ten yards off. In an instant all were out, but the first volley they got killed their Commandant and about 16 men.

One of our waggon men was lying under a waggon, when he saw a woman coming running out of a house towards him. He thought she was going to speak to him, when she shot him.

A Different Age

Members of the Government in 1900 included one duke, three earls, three barons and four marquises. The Labour party was yet to be formed.

Education

In 1900, 50 schools were open. Today that total is under 20. Then, the pupil roll was 1800, now it is 1500. The school-leaving age then was 14, now it is 16.

The 1873 Education Act made education compulsory for all children, but many schools were open long before then, including the **parish schools** and those funded by the **Society for the Propagation of Christian Knowledge**, or the **Gaelic School Society**, or patrons like **Lady Mackenzie** in Gairloch.

The following schools, open in 1900, have closed : **Letterfearn**, **Shiel**, **Dornie** (two including convent school), **Killilan**, **Longard**, **Erbusaig**, **Achmore**, **Attadale**, **Balnacra**, **Craig**, **Lochluichart**, **Strome**, **Kishorn**, **Calnacille**, **Cuaig**, **Arinacrinachd**, **Ardheslaig**, **Alligin**, **Diabaig**, **Opinan**, **Badachro**, **Isle Horisdale**, **Sand**, **Melvaig**, **Mellon Udrigle**, **Laide**, **Badralloch**, **Bordbuie** (Dundonnell), **Strathvaich**, **Inverlael** (Lochbroom), **Ardindrean**, **Loggie**, **Isle Martin**, **Strathcanaird**, **Achduart**, **Tanera Mor**, and **Altandubh**. **Scoraig** closed but re-opened. There were other side-schools (not listed) which served children, even just one child, of families in remote areas, the teacher usually being accommodated by that family.

When Everyone Depended on Fishing

Herring

Fishing was vital in 1900. Some men worked full-time, but most were in the traditional category of crofter-fisherman, and looked to the sea for income when there was little to do on the croft.

Herring fishing, using drift nets, enjoyed a period of relative success in the early years of the century, a time when motive power was beginning to take the place of sail in commercial fishing. The commonest local boats were those of the 'Zulu' design, some built in Wester Ross. These thronged harbours like Ullapool, Gairloch and Kyle when fishing was good.

Some herring was sold direct to German and Russian 'klondyker' ships which visited the Minch each season. Boats from the east coast and Loch Fyne also fished for herring. The Loch Fyne men were specialists in ring-netting, a method locals resented as they believed it caught too many immature fish.

Fishery Board of Scotland statistics for October 1900, the start of the season, recorded good herring catches worth £7,000 in Lochcarron & Skye District, while in Lochbroom landings totalled £5,000, but the quality was higher.

Cod

Another popular method of fishing was the long-line, literally a long fishing-line with thousands of hooks attached. Cod-fishing at Gairloch depended on this method; the success of the cod season between February and April was anxiously awaited. There were fish-curing stations nearby on Eilean Horisdale and Dry Island, which exported cod and saith to Spain, as well as herring to Germany and Russia. The Dry Island station remained open until the end of the First World War when it lost its main export market, Russia, following the Revolution there.

Salmon and Lobsters

Salmon-fishing using bag-nets was another vital activity and there were many netting stations along the coast. The main season was from March to August. Lobsters were caught mainly in autumn and winter. Large numbers of salmon and lobsters were sent by bus and train to Billingsgate market, London.

Fishing was vital not just to earn money but for food. Saith, lythe and herring were especially plentiful. Many people kept a barrel of herring for winter.

On Foot: Before motor travel made life easier, people made light of walking great distances. Kenneth Maclennan recalled his father, head keeper at Strathvaich from 1900, walking twenty miles over the hills to church in Ullapool. Johan MacInnes recalled walking between Attadale and the side-school at Pait, by Loch Monar, where she was the teacher between the wars. Until the late 19th century the Gairloch postman had to walk the length of Loch Maree to and from Kinlochewe on a regular basis.

1900 (continued)

Sgt.John Mackenzie VC

The award of the Victoria Cross in 1900 to John Mackenzie, a native of Lochluichart, brought great pride to Wester Ross. He was fighting with the 2nd Seaforths, attached to the West African Frontier Force in the Ashanti War. His citation was as follows:

On 6th June 1900 at Dompoassi, Sergeant Mackenzie, after working two maxim guns under heavy fire, and being wounded while doing so, volunteered to clear the stockade of the enemy. This he did most gallantly, leading the charge himself, and driving the enemy headlong into the bush.

Mackenzie had joined the Seaforth Highlanders in 1887 at the age of 16. He won nine medals during campaigns in India, Africa and Europe. He was killed in the First World War.

Progress

As the 20th century dawned, great advances in the quality of life were on the horizon - unfortunately a rather distant horizon.

Hydro-electric schemes had already been providing electricity for ten years, motor-cars and lorries were built in Glasgow, and the telephone network was being extended. But the benefits of such progress were slow in coming to Wester Ross. A motor-car would remain a rare sight for many years, and few even had access to a horse or bicycle - so most people accepted the need to walk, often long distances. For heat and light, coal or peat fires and tilly lamps would continue in use in most districts until halfway through the century. There were a few local telephones but, until 1930, the main link with the outside world was still the telegraph.

Church-Building

Underlying the peace of the Sabbath in 1900 was a great sense of change. Less than a decade earlier the Free Presbyterian Church had broken away from the Free Church - now the fresh split in the Free Church led to tension between friends and the eviction of some congregations, mostly those who opted to join the United Free Church. Those made 'homeless' set about planning new churches.

Victorian Values

This was still the Victorian age. The ageing Queen had had a tremendous effect on life in Wester Ross, first by her example in acquiring Balmoral and building her castle - so inspiring other wealthy people to buy estates and build grand houses - and then her visit to Wester Ross in 1877, which did much to popularise the area.

Most major landowners were summer visitors only, without blood ties to the area, and most (though not all) saw their landholdings as mere status symbols. Each estate employed many servants. Vacancies were notified by agencies like Mrs Henry's Servants' Registry in Dingwall, for a range of posts including parlourmaid, tablemaid, dairymaid, laundrymaid, under-maid, cook, kitchenmaid, nurse (i.e. a nanny), and 'boots' (a valet), not forgetting outdoor staff such as gardeners and ghillies. A 'good' salary of £18 per annum (8 shillings a week) was promised to the most responsible staff such as housekeepers and cooks.

Self-Sufficiency

By 1900 the population in every part of Wester Ross had been falling for forty years, in some places for sixty years. Life was really about survival. People aged seventy recalled the time of destitution following the potato famines of the 1840s, seeing relatives and friends forced to emigrate, sometimes literally. There must have been few in Wester Ross who had never considered leaving the area.

People were as self-sufficient as they could be, out of necessity. Clothes were made at home or by local tailors. Crofting and fishing were still vital for putting food on the table.

A source of hope was the Congested Districts Board, now in its fourth year, which acted as a sort of development agency and gave grants to improve land. It also had powers to purchase lands previously cleared of crofters; sadly none in Wester Ross were bought by the time it went out of existence in 1912.

News of the World

Before wireless, television or the internet, newspapers were the main source of information. And there was great demand for news in 1900 as local men were fighting in Africa in the Boer War and Ashanti War.

The *Ross-shire Journal*, like most regional newspapers of that time, covered international, national and local affairs in depth. There was comprehensive coverage of council and public meetings, even of debates at faraway Westminster. The paper showed great deference towards the landed classes, who dominated public life both locally and nationally. Times and attitudes would slowly change.

Lifelines

Sea transport was vital to most Wester Ross communities in 1900, particularly for deliveries of goods and coal. The MacBrayne vessels *Clansman* and *Claymore* were familiar visitors for many years up to the 1930s, carrying both cargo and passengers on their lengthy sailings between Glasgow and Stornoway. Coal 'puffers' called several times a year at most villages.

For people in Applecross, MacBrayne's ferry between Kyle and Stornoway was a vital lifeline, stopping each afternoon at Applecross bay on its way from Kyle, to be met by a local rowing-boat. The ferry also called on the way **to** Kyle in the very early morning, though only in summer. In winter, it was not unknown for passengers trying to get from Applecross to Kyle to make a trip via Stornoway, leaving in the afternoon and getting to Kyle next day.

Other MacBrayne services included the 'swift steamer' which sailed between Oban, Kyle and Gairloch three days a week in summer. There was a Friday service between Kyle, Gairloch, Aultbea and Poolewe, and ferries from Kyle to Portree via Kyleakin and Broadford, and Kyle to Harris and North Uist.

Sea transport was important partly because the roads network was in such terrible shape as the century began. As years went by, calls for improvements were frequent and sometimes desperate.

The railway had extended from Stromeferry to Kyle in 1897. There were horse-coach connections to Ullapool and Gairloch from the railway stations at Garve and Achnasheen.

Main Street, Kyle, in the early years of the century, photographed by Duncan MacPherson. In Gateway to Skye *(1946) he recalled the contrasting views from his pharmacy: from one window, he enjoyed a fine outlook over the sea to Skye, from another the view along Main Street.*

The street showed signs of utter neglect. It was hollowed out with the traffic of years and on wet days, which occurred with a persistence worthy of a better cause, a muddy stream followed a zig-zag course down the centre. This rendered it difficult for any but the well-shod pedestrian to cross, a fact only appreciated by the village shoemaker, a kindly man with a large wife and numerous family to support.

Kyle around the turn of the century

George Washington Wilson

THE CENSUS, 1901

The census of 1901 illustrates some remarkable changes in Wester Ross during the 20th century. As the extracts below show, there were still considerable populations in places now deserted, like Isle Horisdale or Strath na Sealga.

Traditional local names dominated every district, notably the Macraes in Kintail. Almost everyone was native to the Highlands. Most families depended on crofting and fishing, with commerce and domestic service also vital.

Parish Populations

Parish	Population
Glenshiel	343
Kintail	491
Lochalsh	1,830
Lochcarron	1,442
Applecross	1,615
Gairloch	3,797
Lochbroom	3,207
Total	**12,725**

GAELIC
The first language

For the great majority of people living in Wester Ross in 1901, Gaelic was their native tongue, the language spoken at home. Many children only had their first taste of English at school.

The schools, however, for their part discouraged the use of Gaelic, though there were some honourable exceptions.

Most adults spoke some English, as well as Gaelic. But there were many who could speak only Gaelic.

At Toscaig and Uags, for example, all the population (88 people) spoke Gaelic, and of those, nearly a third (26) spoke no English.

This was not unique. In Scotland as a whole, 28,000 people (1 in 200) spoke no English.

230,000 people in Scotland (1 in 20) still spoke Gaelic. That total would fall, by the late 20th century, to just 60,000 (1 in 95).

It is a strange reflection of our times that great efforts are now being made to keep Gaelic alive. The 1901 census, when it confirmed that the number of Gaelic speakers had now ***fallen*** *to 230,000, no doubt gave cause for concern - except to those in government responsible for education.*

Kyle

Kyle had developed rapidly since the railway arrived in 1897. From a small inn and four or five cottages, now the population was 269, including 33 employees of the Highland Railway Co. Others worked for David MacBrayne Ltd, or at the three hotels, banks and shops, while a number of fish-curing businesses had been set up.

Ullapool

Place	Population
Ullapool village	703
Moss	12
Braes	50
TOTAL	**765**

The population of Braes, a crofting township, fell steadily until a private developer built houses in the 1970s.

Dornie & District

Place	Population
Total Population	229
Dornie	88
Bundalloch	77
Carndubh / Carnglass	64

Commonest family names (number of persons)

Name	Persons
Macrae	112
Matheson	16
Macmillan	15
Murchison	15
Macculloch	6
Mackay	5
Mackerlich	5
Mackenzie	5
Maclennan	3

The population included Donald Mackay, priest of the only Roman Catholic church in Wester Ross.

Scoraig

Place	Population
Achmore	36
Lots of Scoraig	57
Scoraig	25
Carnoch	22

Applecross Coast: Airigh-Drishaig to Arinacrinachd

Place	Population
Population	**793**
Airigh-Drishaig	4
Uags	14
Toscaig	88
Crowlin Islands	11
Coillegille	18
Ardban	9
Ard-dhubh	38
Culduie	48
Camusterrach	33
Camusteel	68
Milton	25
Milton Gardens	59
Torgarve	16
Bigton	14
Kirkton	5
Borrodale	17
Keppoch	6
Cruavie	2
Hartfield	2
Salacher	6
Lonbain	48
Calnacille	50
Cuaig	58
Fearnmor	60
Fearnbeg	39
Arinacrinachd	55

Toscaig, Uags & Airigh-Drishaig

Occupations

Crofter	12
Domestic servant	12
Crofter / fisherman	7
Fisherman	4
Sailor	2
Crofter / road contractor	1
Dressmaker	1
Grocer	1
Gamekeeper	1
Own means	1
Retired (crofters)	3

Family names (households)

Name	Households
Gillanders	6
Mackenzie	4
Gordon	3
Kennedy	3
MacDonald	3
Macrae	3
Murchison	2
Beaton	2
MacLean	1
MacLennan	1
Finlayson	1

Remote Living

1. Island Communities

Island	Population
Tanera Mor	71
Isle Martin	33
Isle of Ewe	31
Isle Horisdale	46
Dry Island	8
Crowlin Islands	11
Eilean Ban (E.Gillean)	8

Only Isle of Ewe and Dry Island were inhabited throughout the 20th century. The one family living on Dry Island in 2000 was descended from the last of the island's fish-curers. Tanera was abandoned in 1931 but re-settled.

2. Glens and Straths

Strath na Sealga / Carnmore

Place	Population
Shenavall Lodge	2
Achneigie Lodge	10
Strathnasealga House	7
Carnmore Lodge	8

These were the last families remaining in lands where, before the clearances, a substantial population lived.

__Achneigie__ was inhabited by Roderick Macgregor, a gamekeeper, his wife and their six children. The eldest son, aged 14, was the postman. Also staying with the family was a resident schoolmistress, Mary Ann MacLean, aged 19.

At __Carnmore__ lived Alexander Urquhart, deerstalker, his wife and six sons. The oldest, aged 18, was an under-keeper.

Kintail

Place	Population
Maol-Bhuidhe	3
Pait	5
Iron Lodge	5
Carnach House	5

__Maol-Bhuidhe__, one of the most remote houses in Wester Ross, was the home of James Burnett, a shepherd, his wife and daughter.

Two houses at __Pait__ were occupied by gamekeeper T.Campbell, his wife and daughter, and J.Macrae, an estate worker, and his sister.

__Iron Lodge__ was inhabited by Alexander Mackenzie, a gamekeeper, his wife and sons.

1901

A new Church of Scotland was built in Kyle, where the Institute and Reading Rooms were also opened in January.

An Episcopal Chapel was built by Mr Murray, owner of Lochcarron Estate, within Courthill House, Kishorn. Most of the house was later demolished but the chapel remains in use.

Home Industries Exhibition

The first South-West Ross Highland Home Industries Exhibition was held at Duncraig Castle. The exhibition was to become an important annual showcase for locally produced goods such as tweeds and woollens. It was held again at Duncraig in 1902, then at Kyle from 1903 to 1905, and at Lochcarron in 1906. The Highland Home Industries Society encouraged such exhibitions in many areas, the Inverness event being of particular importance.

The West Highland Railway between Fort William and Mallaig opened. It was significant for Wester Ross in that it represented competition to the Kyle line for the all-important west-coast fish trade. The Kyle-Stornoway steamer service was now extended to link Kyle with Mallaig.

Celebrations for an Heir

In December 1901, the pupils of Ullapool School were treated to a celebration tea in honour of the 21st birthday of the "heir to the Ullapool property", Lieutenant Matheson.

Matheson, who was then serving in the war in South Africa, was the son of Major Matheson of the Lews, to whom a telegram was sent on the pupils' behalf. "Children of Ullapool School heartily thank Mrs Matheson and yourself for splendid treat provided for them today, congratulate you on Lieutenant Matheson's majority, wish him safe return from South Africa, long life and happiness."

After tea 'with a double supply of fruit', pupils sang the National Anthem. That evening, feuars and tenants of the village met for another celebration at the Royal Hotel, where there was a firework display. A second telegram was sent. Both events were organised by Kenneth Cameron, estate factor for the Mathesons, who would remain lairds of Ullapool until 1918.

The 1900s

Mr Mackenzie of Garve Hotel leased the Royal Hotel in Ullapool. He operated a coach service between the two hotels.

Diabaig pier was built.

The Congested Districts Board offered a grant of 25% (£320) towards building a road from Badcaul to Badluarach, and £333 for another new road from Achnahaird to Altandubh in Coigach.

Two preventive officers based at Ullapool, while making a search of remote Priest Island in June, confiscated a whisky still which they found "hidden in an almost inaccessible position."

The Boer War ended on 31st May.

The first hydro-electric scheme in Ross-shire was inaugurated on Ben Wyvis by the Strathpeffer & Dingwall Electricity Supply Co, generating 80 kw of power.

There was shock in Ross-shire and throughout the Highlands when General Sir Hector MacDonald, war hero and most famous son of the county, was found shot dead in his hotel room in Paris. He had committed suicide after suffering from depression following allegations of corrupt behaviour. The MacDonald monument which now stands on the hillside above Dingwall was erected by public subscription in 1907.

Lord Middleton, owner of the Applecross estate, visited townships along the North Applecross coast by yacht in September, giving each community a stag.

The British home fleet visited Loch Broom in October.

At a meeting of the Ullapool Nursing Committee, Lady Fowler of Braemore took it upon herself to make up the annual subsidy paid by the Committee to the nurses in the district, ensuring they each received a salary of £15 (5s.8d. a week).

An unusually large shoal of herrings in Loch Ewe gave good fishing to local boats in October, with about 100 crans (c.100,000 herring) landed on each shore.

John Mackenzie VC of Lochluichart was promoted to Captain with the Royal Scots. He had previously been promoted to Lieutenant in the Black Watch in 1900, after 13 years with the Seaforths.

Ledgowan Lodge was built.

Flowerdale House, home of Sir Kenneth and Lady Mackenzie, Gairloch Estate, was extended. They also owned Conan House in Easter Ross where they spent the winter (as the family still does).

Gairloch Golf Club was revived in April after a short lapse in activity.

An illicit still was seized at Laide.

A disused copper mine at Kishorn was re-opened and worked for a short time.

An exhibition and sale arranged by the Northern Gairloch Home Industries Association was held at Drumchork.

On 30th September, King Edward VII visited Loch Duich, coming ashore at Letterfearn. He paid a return visit the following year.

Aultbea Pier was re-opened in October after being repaired at the expense of the local proprietor, the Earl of Zetland.

A fishing-boat with a crew of three local men was lost off Aultbea.

The steamer *Sheila* took over the Kyle-Stornoway ferry service.

During a fierce storm in January, 24 fishing vessels including eight from Stornoway were driven aground in Loch Broom. Most were badly damaged.

A new Caledonian Bank building was opened in Kyle, and a branch of the Commercial Bank was opened in Dornie.

Electric cables were struck by lightning during a fierce storm around Strathpeffer in June. Inverness was provided with electricity under a private scheme, later taken over by the Town Council.

The station clerk at Achnasheen was killed when he fell between two carriages.

The terrible condition of roads in Lochbroom, in particular the section of the main road between Braemore and the head of Loch Broom, was discussed by the Mid-Ross District Committee of the County Council. A lady had complained of being severely jolted while travelling by coach along the road to Ullapool. It was noted that the local timber trade was causing damage to the road on that section. The District Committee suggested that the parish of Lochbroom should form itself into a 'special roads district' and approach the Congested Districts Board for funding to repair the road. Funds were eventually found to repair the Ullapool-Garve road the following year.

Shieldaig was given a water supply by Mr Murray of Lochcarron Estate.

The Northern Gairloch Industrial Association organised an exhibition of Highland Home Industries at Poolewe.

Gairloch School Board decided that, when appointing teachers in future, they would give preference to Gaelic-speakers if all other factors and qualifications were equal.

Mr Mackenzie of Dundonnell Estate paid for pupils of Badcaul School to be given a cup of hot cocoa every day in winter.

Three fishermen from Fearnmore were drowned in Loch Torridon after their boat capsized in a gale.

Film Treat

Mr Munro, cinematographist of Dingwall, who is always welcome in the district, paid his usual visit to Kishorn last week when he gave a delightful entertainment in the Public School.

Ross-shire Journal, 10th January 1908

1907

Achtercairn Secondary School, Gairloch, was downgraded in status to Junior Secondary School. This meant that, after their third year at Achtercairn, pupils wishing to continue their education would have to do so at Dingwall Academy.

The Postmaster-General, replying to a request for a six-days-per-week postal delivery in Coigach, said it would only be possible in July, August and September - which was the existing arrangement. The rest of the year, the mail cart left Ullapool on alternate days only, returning the next.

Shiel Inn, at Shiel Bridge by the head of Loch Duich, closed after serving travellers for nearly 200 years. It was to be used as a shooting lodge in future.

Millionaire's Visit

Mr and Mrs Andrew Carnegie and their daughter passed through Ullapool on their way to see the Corrie-Hallie Falls, Braemore, on Saturday. They had luncheon at the Caledonian Hotel. Mr Carnegie spoke a few words to some people who had come to the corner of the hotel to see the millionaire.

Ross-shire Journal, July

Lochcarron's Free Presbyterian Church was built.

Local volunteer companies were designated as units in the Territorial Army. The 1st Company, Ross-shire Artillery Volunteers, based in Lochcarron, re-formed as part of the Ross Mountain Battery, 4th (Highland) Mountain Brigade. Local companies of the 1st Ross-shire Rifle (Ross Highland) Volunteers, which had been affiliated to the Seaforth Highlanders since 1887, became part of the 4th Battalion, Seaforth Highlanders (Ross & Cromarty) (the Gairloch Volunteers became D Company and the Ullapool Volunteers E Company).

Lochcarron Golf Club was formed, and the new course was in play by 1909. The club has continued in existence, apart from occasional periods around war-time. Balmacara golf course was also opened that year, but has long since closed.

Motoring Accident

A chauffeur from the Culag Hotel, Lochinver was killed after his Arrol-Johnston car crashed near Rhegreanoch on the narrow coast road between Inverpolly and Assynt. His passenger, a guest at the hotel, had been picked up at Ullapool, and later stated he was surprised the chauffeur had chosen that route instead of the more usual road via Knockan.

Gairloch herring fishermen had good catches in Loch Broom at the start of the season in November, which they landed at the fishing-stations of Badachro.

A committee of Gairloch residents approached David MacBrayne Ltd for improvements on the regular steamer services to Glasgow and Stornoway. In 1909 it was reported that the steamer *Unicorn* was now making daily trips between Gairloch and Kyle.

Lord and Lady Lovelace of Ben Damph Estate supplied tenants and servants with a gift of venison before returning south for the winter. This was reported to be the thirteenth year in succession they had done this.

Ullapool's new Free Church was built on Quay Street. The original Free Church on Mill Street had become the United Free Church at the turn of the century.

Gairloch Parish Church was reconstructed, with a new bellcote added.

At the end of the herring-fishing season in February, the total catch in Loch Broom was a record 40,000 crans. Most landings were made from October to December. The cod-fishing at Gairloch was less successful, with catches down a half by the season's end in April.

Choosing a Chief

Rival claims to be recognised as chief of Clan Macrae, by the leaders of the Macraes of Inverinate and Macraes of Conchra, were assessed by the Lord Lyon King of Arms in 1909, who decided in favour of the Inverinate line. But he need hardly have bothered, as the Macraes of Conchra continued to recognise only their own Sir Colin Macrae.

Duncraig Castle about 1900, with Plockton in the background. The Castle, built by Sir Alexander Matheson in 1866, was then still the home of the Matheson family. Later owners gave it to the County Council in 1945, to be used as a domestic science college. After the college's closure in 1989 the building lay empty throughout the 1990s.

(Photograph by Sir Roderick Matheson from Sir Torquhil Matheson's collection with the permission of Lady Serena Matheson)

Arrivals at Inverness Station about 1906. A few travellers might be bound for estates in Wester Ross, but most were probably going no further than Inverness or Strathpeffer Spa

Celebrating the Old New Year

A' Challuinn. *Thursday 13th January was observed as New Year's Day, Old Style, in most parts of the parish of Gairloch. The day was spent in the traditional functions of visiting and greeting friends, Fingalian feasting, singing Gaelic songs, and games of shinty. All the schools and places of business were closed. The children on the previous day, as usual, went their rounds with their bags and camans singing their Calluinn duans.*

Ross-shire Journal, 14th January 1910

A local minister later recalled that this custom continued at Gairloch until the end of the First World War.

General Election

On 27th January, polling day for the first of two general elections held in 1910, the *Ross-shire Journal* reported that, despite heavy snowfall at Ullapool 'the electors in the outlying districts, such as shepherds and keepers, came in to a man'.

Cod-fishing at Gairloch

A sudden upturn in the cod fishery at Gairloch was reported in March. Thirty boats worked cod-nets and had catches ranging from 50 to 250 cod over three days. Two line boats working great lines were reported to have got plenty of herring bait but were restricted in their catches by stormy weather.

A Medical Officer for schools in Ross shire was appointed for the first time.

Lairds and Ladies

A good relationship with tenants on their estates was a matter of concern to most landowners, at least for public show. Many invited local children to Christmas entertainments. Some, like the Reids at New Kelso, organised special events such as a hyacinth show at Lochcarron in 1910.

The comings and goings of lairds and their families were faithfully reported by the local press. This example is from the *Ross-shire Journal* for 6th May.

Sir Arthur and Lady Bignold of Lochrosque are enjoying a fishing holiday in Wales. Sir Arthur will probably return to London before coming north for the season. Lady Anne Murray of Lochcarron passed through Dingwall on Friday on her way south.

Diary of a Year

1910

Whooping Cough Alarm

An outbreak in Lochbroom led to Ullapool Higher Grade School closing indefinitely.

New Drill Hall for Kinlochewe

The work of erecting the Drill Hall is proceeding apace. Acting upon a suggestion from the Adjutant, a committee has been formed for the purpose of using the hall as a reading and writing room. Till now there was no place where the young people could gather together of an evening. Putting stone, throwing hammer and jumping sticks have also been given to the section, and are much appreciated.

Ross-shire Journal, 29th April 1910

New Churches

United Free Churches were built at Shieldaig and at Lochcarron, where the congregation had been evicted from the Free Church some years earlier and forced to worship outdoors at first before finding temporary accommodation. (The UF church is now the parish church.)

In The Outside World

Tension grew between Britain and Germany, as huge fleets of ships were built in both countries.

Two General Elections were held during 1910. In the first, there was a dead heat (Liberals 273, Tories 273), but the 43 Labour MPs supported the Liberals, as did 82 Irish Nationalists. In the second, there was another dead heat: 272-272, with two seats gained by the Irish Nationalists.

Suffragettes were in the news in 1910, being regularly imprisoned or given hard labour.

Other political topics included the rights and wrongs of the House of Lords being allowed to overrule decisions of the House of Commons.

Croft Experiments

A lecturer from the North of Scotland Agricultural College visited Poolewe and Inverasdale to set up experiments in improving drainage, croft management etc. Typical crofts were selected for various tests in gowing cereals, potatoes and turnips. It was hoped the experiments would be of practical benefit and also of interest to senior pupils in local schools.

Illicit Distilling

Preventive staff (or excisemen) based at Ullapool discovered a smuggling bothy while searching moors above Badluarach, Little Lochbroom in May, which they demolished, along with the utensils found. The bothy was described as 'well furnished and very substantially built, dug out of the moss to a depth of many feet, the roof being on a level with the surroundings and skilfully concealed with heather.' There was evidence that it had recently been in use.

Popular Laird Dies

The death in June of Duncan Darroch, laird of Torridon, caused great sadness. As a mark of respect, a party of 100 local men carried his body on the first part of its journey to a final resting-place at Gourock.

Puffers at Badachro

Among a number of arrivals in July were the *Smiling Morn* with coal, and *Warfinger* with salt, both for Mr J.Mackenzie. Another delivery of coal, for Mr Gunn, was made by the steamer *Lady of the Lake*.

Appeal for emigrants

(advert)

Canadian Pacific. Direct service from Great Britain to and through Canada by magnificent Empress steamers and comfortable express trains. Special care taken of women and children emigrants. For particulars, apply to Canadian Pacific Railway, Glasgow, or local agents everywhere.

Ross-shire Journal, 7th January

The British Emigrants' Information Office advertised vacancies in Canada for farmers and farm labourers, and for strong men for railway construction in the Western provinces at two dollars a day. Shepherds were required in the Western United States, where women were also needed for domestic service. Many men from Wester Ross emigrated to Montana.

Postal Services by Motor

At a meeting of Lochbroom Parish Council, chairman Kenneth Cameron submitted a resolution which was unanimously adopted.

The Parish Council earnestly urge upon the Postmaster-General the great necessity of conveying the mails from Garve to Ullapool by motor car instead of by horse carriage at present. The district to be served is one of growing importance, especially with the yearly herring fishing at Ullapool. The Council are very strongly of opinion that this district is not receiving the same treatment in the matter of the mail service as the districts in Sutherlandshire, where the service has been conducted by motor car for several years.

More Motoring Matters

Later in the year it was reported that the Ullapool-Garve road was in such a poor state that motor-cars were having great difficulty negotiating steep climbs and passengers having to get out and walk.

Garage facilities and car hire (with chauffeur) were now available at several hotels.

Baptised in the Cave at Cove

In July, the *Ross-shire Journal* reported on a recent service in the church cave at Cove. Mr Mackinnon, the Free Church minister at Gairloch, had baptised four children in front of a large congregation. *Many years ago this cave was fitted up with a small pulpit and seats, and religious meetings used to be conducted by the late Mr William Urquhart, catechist. Since his death about twelve years ago, no service has been held there. The last baptism was administered some twenty years ago by the late Rev. Ronald Dingwall.*

Miss Lang, headmistress at Inverlael Public School, Lochbroom, retired after 19 years. In addition to her teaching duties she was the local postmistress.

Parish Values 1910-11

	Acres	Rateable value
Lochbroom	261,020	£13,858
Gairloch	200,646	£11,928
Applecross	109,293	£4,385
Lochcarron	85,090	£7,053
Lochalsh	49,532	£5,634
Kintail	77,441	£3,919
Glenshiel	57,320	£3,367
Total	840,342	£50,144

Street Lighting for Kyle

At a meeting in the Institute in October, a committee was appointed to examine the costs of installing street lights in Kyle. Enough funds were raised to erect seven lamps. At this time, a community could declare itself a 'special lighting district' in order to qualify for grants to erect lights, whether gas or electric.

Poolewe Gaelic Concert

Poolewe Gaelic Choir gave a concert in the local school in September. Lord Mackenzie, Inveran Lodge, presided, and a large audience attended, including many strangers "who were struck with the beautiful Gaelic music submitted".

The annual Exhibition of Highland Village Industries was held at Plockton. Hand-worked articles on sale included tweeds, woollens, socks, knickerbockers, kilt hose, underclothing and bedcovers, along with vegetables, dairy produce, dyes and carvings.

Construction of Rubha Reidh Lighthouse began in autumn 1910. The light came into service in January 1912, with three keepers and their families sharing accommodation next to the lighthouse. The only access was by sea. It was not until 1962 that the Northern Lighthouse Board provided a road to Rubha Reidh.

The Salmon-Fishing

Some 25 salmon-fishing stations operated in Wester Ross in the early years of the 20th century. There were four in Coigach alone, at Badenscallie, Badentarbet, Reiff and Achnahaird, each employing about thirty men in the season, which was usually from May to August.

In spring, after the peats were cut, local crofters would turn to the salmon fishing. Each station worked several bag-nets, and at each there was a bothy where the men would often stay while the season was in full swing.

The decline in salmon-netting in later years was due to several factors, most importantly the decline in numbers of salmon. But the work was also traditionally handed down from father to son and lost its appeal with some of the younger generation. Students were taken on in several districts such as Coigach latterly, and several neighbouring stations worked by one team.

The Herring-Fishing

Early in the season, in the first week of November, good fishing at Gairloch was reported by the *Ross-shire Journal*.

A few local boats did very well. Boats are from all quarters, from Campbeltown to Leith. With two Glasgow steamers buying on Friday and Saturday, Badachro Harbour presented a lively appearance.

The season was also well under way at Ullapool, with 180 boats fishing. Landings already totalled 5,600 crans, four times more than in 1909. A cran was roughly 1000 fish; 5,600 crans represented five million herrings!

The main herring season in Wester Ross at this time lasted from October to March. Each season, local crews were joined by others from the north-east and south-west (Kintyre and Ayrshire). The east-coast fishermen, like the locals, were drift-netters, while those from the south-west preferred ring-netting, a method involving two boats forming a circle with a net, rather than towing a chain of nets as in drift-netting. However, ring-netting was resented in the West Highlands because locals believed it caught too many immature fish. The Kintyre and Ayrshire men often used drift-nets in this area to avoid trouble. In 1908, boats belonging to ring-netters were smashed up by angry drift-net fishermen at Ullapool.

Herring fishing was always done at night. Angus Martin in *The North Minch Fishermen* described the uncanny skill of the best fishermen, who could identify where herring were at dead of night by hearing the sound of a shoal moving through the water.

Representing the People

Wester Ross and South-West Ross were represented by 13 councillors on Ross and Cromarty County Council in 1910. Most councillors were major landowners - and some were absentee lairds. Major Blunt-Mackenzie of Castle Leod, Strathpeffer, represented his own west-coast estate of Coigach, even though he did not live there. Murdo Mackenzie of Ardross lived on the east coast but represented Dundonnell. Others were resident, such as Osgood Mackenzie, Inverewe, and Sir Kenneth Mackenzie, Gairloch.

WHO DID WHAT IN WESTER ROSS IN 1911

Commercial services 90 years ago included crafts and trades which have long disappeared from the area: for example, there were fifteen blacksmiths. Some people had several trades: grocer & postmaster was a common combination. Almost everyone crofted and fished as well, so many people had three or four occupations. The source is Slater's Directory.

Medical Services were provided by seven doctors (parochial medical officers). These were Dr Macrae, Balmacara; Dr Mackay, Lochcarron; Dr Lucas, Applecross; Dr Calder, Torridon; Dr Knox, Gairloch; Dr Macnaughton, Poolewe; Dr Gunn, Ullapool.

Police The county police force had a strength of 52 men (including Lewis). There were 9 single-manned stations, at Achiltibuie, Ullapool, Aultbea, Gairloch, Shieldaig, Applecross, Lochcarron, Kyle and Dornie. The only sergeant was at Kyle.

Post Offices 36 post offices served even very small communities like Nostie and Achanalt. Those in larger villages offered a telegraph and money-order service.

Banks There were seven banks: two at Kyle (Commercial Bank, Bank of Scotland), one each at Ardelve, Dornie, Lochcarron, Gairloch, and Ullapool.

Hotels There were 24 hotels: at Cluanie, Ardelve *(Aird Ferry)*, Balmacara, Kyle *(three)*, Plockton, Stromeferry, Strathcarron, Lochcarron, Applecross, Shieldaig, Achnasheen, Achanalt, Kinlochewe, Loch Maree, Gairloch *(two)*, Poolewe, Aultbea, Dundonnell, Ullapool *(two)*, and Achiltibuie. Also an inn at Totaig.

Schools There were 48 board schools (and also side-schools: these not listed opposite).

Churches 37 churches & 30 ministers: 13 Established, 9 United Free, 9 Free, 5 Free Presbyterian, 1 Roman Catholic.

Farms There were 56 farms (as opposed to crofts). Gairloch had 17, Lochbroom 9, Lochcarron 9, Lochalsh 6, Kintail 6, Applecross 3, Glenshiel 3, Lochluichart 3.

Businesses & Trades, Laide to Kinlochewe

Aultbea/Laide/Coast (10)	
H.Cameron	joiner & postmaster
G.Forbes	stonemason, Coast
B.Mackenzie	grocer, Sand
D.Mackenzie	stonemason
J.Mackenzie	tailor, Laide
J.Mackenzie	grocer & draper, Laide
K.Mackenzie	weaver, Mellon Charles
R.Mackenzie	blacksmith, Laide
W.Mackenzie	grocer & draper
C.Mackenzie	hotelkeeper *Aultbea*
Poolewe (7)	
H.Mackenzie	grocer
J.Mackenzie	miller, Boor
J.MacLean	blacksmith
A.MacLennan (Mrs)	hotelkeeper
Urquhart & MacLennan	tailors
R.MacLennan	tailor
B.Ross	carpenter
Inverasdale (4)	
M.MacLean	grocer & postmaster
J.Macleod	weaver
M.Macleod	weaver
A.Macpherson	boot/shoe-maker
Strath (9)	
R.Forbes	miller
R.MacIntyre	grocer & draper
J.MacIver	grocer
A.Mackenzie	joiner
D.Mackenzie	tailor
H.Mackintosh	blacksmith
C.MacLean	butcher
K.MacLean	joiner & wheelwright
W.Ross & Son	tailors
Gairloch (7)	
J.Bain	bootmaker
J.Campbell	photographer
W.Fraser	estate carpenter
Gunn Bros	bakers/grocers, Charlestown
K.Macrae	grocer/draper, Aultgrishan
Powrie & Co.	salmon fishing lessees
A.&A.Burgess	bank agents
Port Henderson (1)	
J.Mackenzie	boat-builder
Badachro (8)	
R.Gunn	fish-curer
A.Mackenzie	fish-curer
R.Taylor	fish-curer
D.MacCallum	grocer & draper
J.Mackenzie	beer retailer
J.C.Mackenzie	grocer
MacLean & Co.	grocers & drapers
R.Macrae	tailor
Loch Maree / Kinlochewe (6)	
A.Robertson	hotels *L.Maree & Kinlochewe*
A.MacIver	blacksmith
P.Mackenzie	grocer & postmaster
W.Mackenzie	grocer
K.&W.MacLennan	tailors
A.Macrae	boot/shoe-maker

Applecross to Torridon

Applecross (5)	
John Macdonald	stonemason
John MacLean	boot-maker
Duncan Macleod	grocer
Alexander Macrae	grocer & postmaster
Duncan Murchison	grocer
Milltown (3)	
Kenneth Ferguson	blacksmith
Murdo Gillanders	tailor
Donald Livingston	grocer
Shieldaig (7)	
Hector Grant	grocer / draper & registrar
Alex Livingstone	shopkeeper
Dugald Livingstone	shopkeeper
Mary Ann MacLean	hotelkeeper *Temperance*
Kenneth Maclennan	tailor
Donald Macrae	grocer
Roderick Macrae	grocer
Annat (2)	
Donald Mackenzie	grocer & draper
William Mackenzie	mason
Torridon (1)	
Duncan MacLean	grocer
Alligin (1)	
Donald Macdonald	grocer & postmaster
Inveralligin (1)	
Murdo Macdonald	boat-builder
Diabaig (2)	
John Macpherson	grocer
John Maclennan	grocer

Businesses and Trades in Lochalsh

Kyle (20)	
H.Mackay	fish-curer
D.Macrae	fish-curer
D.Stewart	fish-curer
Murchison/Stewart	fish-curers
M.Stewart	fish salesman
D.Macrae	tailor
D.MacLean	shoe-maker
J.Fraser	painter
D.MacGregor	grocer/draper
A.Macrae	grocer/draper
M.Macrae	grocer/draper
R.Macrae	grocer
Mrs C Fraser	laundry
D.Urquhart	hotel *Kyle*
R.MacLeod	hotel *Temperance*
H.Ward	hotel *Station*
Hossack/Campbell	bank agents
T.Kitson	bank agent
N.Macintosh	steamer agent
D.Wallace	lighthouse
Ardelve (7)	
D.Cameron	hotel *Aird Ferry*
A.Campbell	mail contractor
D.Macdonald	blacksmith
A.Macrae	butcher
D.Macrae	blacksmith
J.Macrae	grocer/draper
J.Macrae (Miss)	grocer & post
Balmacara (7)	
J.MacLennan	steamer agent
J.Mackenzie	blacksmith, Reraig
A.Sinclair	hotel *Balmacara*
K.Murchison	grocer
A.Matheson	grocer
F.Macrae	grocer
J.MacLennan	carpenter
Erbusaig (1)	
A.Macrae (Mrs)	grocer
Duirinish (3)	
A.MacAulay	butcher
M.MacLennan	grocer
D.Cameron	butcher
Plockton (6)	
J.Aitken	carpenter
J.Fraser	slater
J.Mackenzie	carpenter
J.Mackenzie	tailor
D.Macrae	innkeeper
F.Macrae	grocers
Stromeferry (1)	
D.Macdonald	grocer / post

Businesses & Trades, Glenshiel

J.Boyd	innkeeper, *Cluanie Inn*
R.Matheson	innkeeper, *Totaig Inn*
M.Macrae	grocer, Letterfearn
R.MacLennan	tailor, Letterfearn
G.Grant (Miss)	grocer & draper, Shiel
E.Macrae	grocer, Carngorm

Businesses & Trades, Kintail

A.MacLennan	tailor, Carndhu
A.Macrae	carpenter, Bundalloch
C.Macrae	boat-builder, Bundalloch
J.Finlayson	boat-builder, Dornie
F.Fraser	joiner
A.Macrae	stone mason
D.Macrae	blacksmith
D.Macrae	boot/shoe-maker
J.Macrae	tailor
K.Macrae (Miss)	grocer
B.Matheson (Miss)	grocer *(also registrar)*
F.Matheson	grocer

Businesses & Trades, Lochcarron

Strathcarron (6)

J.Finlayson	carpenter
B.Kennedy (Mrs)	grocer
J.Macrae	boot/shoe-maker
BK.Macrae (Miss)	milliner
K.Murchison	blacksmith, New Kelso
W.Mackenzie	hotelkeeper, *Station*

Lochcarron (Jeantown) (24)

R.Sinclair	bank agent
K.Cameron	carpenter
J.Carruthers	plumber
D.Forbes	shoe-maker
R.Gollan	carpenter, Slumbay
A.Mackenzie	grocer, Slumbay
D.MacLean	stonemason, Slumbay
J.Hall	painter
B.Kennedy (Mrs)	grocer & shoe dealer
J.Macdonald	tailor
M.Macdonald	grocer
A.Mackay	tailor
A.Mackenzie	tailor
F.Mackenzie	boot/shoe-maker
J.Mackenzie	carpenter
J.Mackenzie	baker & grocer
K.Mackenzie	carrier
R.Mackenzie	cattle dealer
S.Mackenzie	tailor
D.MacLennan	butcher
R.MacLennan	butcher
J.Morrison	hotelkeeper, *Lochcarron*
D.Polson	shopkeeper / cattle dealer
J.Stewart	stonemason

Ardaneaskan (1)

D.Macrae	boat-builder

Kishorn & Achintraid (4)

W.Gordon	blacksmith
N.Macrae	grocer
K.Murchison (Mrs)	grocer
F.Macrae	tailor / postmaster

Local Schools and Teachers

Letterfearn	*Mr Purdie*
Shiel	*vacant 1911*
Inverinate	*Miss Munro*
Killilan	*Mr Graham*
Dornie	*Mr MacLeod*
Auchtertyre	*Mr Macrae*
Kyle	*Mr Urquhart*
Erbusaig	*Miss Butter*
Plockton	*Mr Sorlie*
Achmore	*Miss Mackay*
Attadale	*Miss Macleish*
Lochcarron	*Mr MacLennan*
Balnacra	*Miss Mackay*
Kishorn	*Miss Stewart*
Applecross	*Mr Macdonald*
Calnacille	*Miss Mackenzie*
Cuaig	*Mr Macrae*
Ardheslaig	*Miss McLennan*
Shieldaig	*Miss Mackenzie*
Torridon	*Miss Peace*
Alligin	*Mr MacPhail*
Diabaig	*Mr Macmartin*
Kinlochewe	*Miss Band*
Achnasheen	*Mr Duff*
Lochluichart	*Miss Mackenzie*
Strathvaich	*Miss Grant*
Opinan	*Mr Mackenzie*
Isle Horisdale	*Miss Macpherson*
Achtercairn	*Mr Macgillivray*
Sand	*Mrs Calder*
Melvaig	*Mr Young*
Poolewe	*Mr Cameron*
Inverasdale	*Mr Rankine*
Bualnaluib	*Mr Kerr*
Laide	*Mrs Summers*
Mellon Udrigle	*Miss Campbell*
Badcaul	*Mrs Hagarty*
Badralloch	*Miss MacAulay*
Scoraig	*Mrs Macgregor*
Ardindrean	*Miss Campbell*
Lochbroom	*Mr Bathgate*
Ullapool	*Mr Cameron*
Isle Martin	*Miss Cameron*
Strathcanaird	*Miss Gunn*
Achduart	*Miss MacLeod*
Achiltibuie	*Mr Mackenzie*
Altandubh	*Mrs MacIver*
Tanera Mor	*Miss Fraser*

Businesses & Trades, Lochbroom

Dundonnell (6)

M.Cameron	blacksmith
J.Urquhart	hotelkeeper, *Dundonnell*
D.Mackenzie	carpenter, Ardessie
R.MacLean	grocer & stonemason
I.Mackenzie (Mrs)	grocer, Durnamuck
A.Mackenzie	grocer, Badluarach

Scoraig & Badralloch (4)

J.Macdonald	grocer, Badralloch
K.Macrae	stonemason, Scoraig
K.&J.MacIver	grocers, Scoraig
S.Mackenzie	cattle dealer, Scoraig

Lochbroom (5)

J.Cameron	shoe-maker, Crofton
D.Mackenzie	blacksmith, Crofton
W.Sinclair	estate forester, Glackour
A.Mackenzie	grocer, Ardindrean
D.Campbell	tailor, Ardcharnich

Ullapool (60)

W.Aird	watch & clock-maker
Cameron & Co	woollen manufacturers
J.Cameron (Mrs)	grocer
K.Cameron	grocer & baker
K.Cameron	steamer agent (& factor)
D.&J.Campbell	coal merchants
J.Campbell	joiner
I.Dawson (Mrs)	nurse
T.Dawson	stonemason
D.Fraser	general merchant
J.Harrison	grocer
Kennett & Macmillan	painters
W.Laurence	general merchant
D.Mackay	baker
H.Mackay	tailor
J.MacNeill	coastguard
A.Macdonald	boot-maker
M.Macdonald	cabinet-maker
D.Macewer	tailor
D.Mackenzie	grocer
D.Mackenzie	miller
F.Mackenzie	carpenter
G.Mackenzie	carpenter
H.Mackenzie	gocer & draper
H.Mackenzie	bank agent
I.Mackenzie (Miss)	dressmaker
J.Mackenzie (Mrs)	spirit dealer
J.Mackenzie	stonemason
J.Mackenzie	tailor
K.Mackenzie	grocer & butcher
K.Mackenzie	stonemason
K.Mackenzie	butcher
L.Mackenzie	baker
L.Mackenzie	carter
M.Mackenzie	carpenter
M.Mackenzie	grocer
J.Mackenzie (Mrs)	newsagent
R.Mackenzie	tailor
W.Mackenzie	hotelkeeper *Royal*
A.MacLean	grocer
J.MacLean	tailor
M.MacLean	ferryman & spirit dealer
M.MacLean	stonemason
A.MacLeod	blacksmith
A.MacLeod (Mrs)	dressmaker
D.MacLeod	blacksmith
H.Macrae	cattle dealer
J. & K.Macrae	boot/shoe-makers
D.Matheson	grocer
D.Matheson	carrier
G.Morrison	hotelkeeper *Caledonian*
W.Murdie	butcher
Ross & Sons	grocers
J.Ross	stonemason
K.Ross	tailor
W.Stewart	shoe-maker
Ullapool Meat Co	butchers
J.Urquhart	cattle dealer
M.Urquhart	tailor
W.Whyte	baker

Coigach (26)

A.Campbell	flour dealer
J.Campbell (Mrs)	grocer
R.Campbell	merchant
R.Fraser	grocer *(& registrar)*
W.Fraser	flour dealer
K.Graham	joiner
M.Gray	merchant, Altandubh
A.Mackenzie (Mrs)	shopkeeper, Badenscallie
J.Mackenzie	tailor, Badenscallie
R.Mackenzie	joiner
A.MacLean	bootmaker, Altandubh
J.MacLean	shoemaker, Altandubh
K.MacLean	boat-builder, Altandubh
J.MacLeod	merchant, Polbain
M.MacLeod (Mrs)	shopkeeper, Polbain
M.MacLeod	bootmaker, Achnahaird
M.&N.MacLeod	stonemason, Polbain
R.MacLeod	cattle dealer
R.MacLeod	tailor, Polglass
W.MacLeod	blacksmith, Polglass
W.MacLeod	shopkeeper, Polbain
A.Matheson	grocer & postmaster
G.Matheson (Mrs)	grocer
H.Morrison	hotelkeeper *Achiltibuie*
W.Muir	merchant
W.Rae	salmon fishings lessee

The main occupations in 1911 were, of course, still crofting and fishing. The various farms employed labourers and shepherds. Some farms belonged to estates, who also employed managers, outdoor staff, and domestic servants. Many men worked for the Highland Railway Company, some for MacBrayne's at Kyle. There were local mail-coach operators, and the GPO employed postmen in addition to postmasters listed overleaf. The hotels listed overleaf also employed staff.

Other Occupations in 1911

Public services provided considerable employment, though nothing like as much as today. As well as fifty or so teachers employed by parish school boards, there were *Inland Revenue Officers* based at Lochcarron and Gairloch and two *Fishery Officers* at Ullapool. Five *Customs & Excise Officers* were based at Gairloch and Ullapool, including three 'preventive men' to stop smuggling.

Eleven *Registrars of Births, Deaths & Marriages* were employed, serving Glenshiel, Kintail, Lochalsh, Lochcarron, Applecross, Shieldaig, Gairloch South, Gairloch North, Lochbroom, Coigach, and Lochluichart.

There were *Inspectors of Poor* for South West Ross (Mr Mackintosh), Lochcarron (Mr Campbell), Applecross (Mr Mackenzie), Gairloch (Mr Macrae), and Lochbroom (Mr Ross). These also acted as clerks to their parish councils. Collectors of Rates served the same areas: Mrs Gray, Mr Macrae, Mr Gillanders, Mr Macrae and Mr Ross. The last two were also Inspectors of Poor.

The County Council employed two *Road Surveyors*: one covered the Western District and lived at Slattadale, the other covered the South-West District and lived at Inverinate. The County Council, of course, also employed local contractors and roadmen to maintain the roads.

Four *Drill Instructors* were employed to train local Territorial Force companies. These were the 2nd Lovat Scouts, E Squadron, based at Kyle, the Ross Mountain Battery at Lochcarron, and the 4th Seaforth Highlanders, D & E companies, at Gairloch and Ullapool respectively.

Above: Ledgowan House, built in 1904, was one of several private shooting lodges to re-open as a hotel later in the century

Below: Rhu Dubh (Black Point), Wester Slumbay, Lochcarron around the turn of the century

End of Peace

1911

Gairloch School Board announced plans to build a new school at Badachro. The Board also declared a week's holiday in honour of the Coronation of George V, each pupil to be given a Coronation Bible.

The Commercial Bank opened new premises at Dornie. The people of Dornie also raised funds for a village hall.

The Congested Districts Board gave a grant of £105 (75% of the cost) for a road to Cove on the west shore of Loch Ewe.

Two people were killed in an accident in May when a Talbot car belonging to the Loch Maree Hotel left the road by Loch a' Chroisg near Achnasheen. The victims were the chauffeur and a woman from Gairloch.

A motor-bus replaced the horse-drawn stage-coach on the Ullapool-Garve service.

Ullapool Pier Trustees, constituted the previous year, opened their new pier.

The first Lochbroom Crofters' Cattle Show was held at Achiltibuie.

Aeroplane flights were an attraction for visitors to Strathpeffer Highland Games.

In December Dingwall Academy was closed due to an epidemic of scarlet fever.

Mabel's Last Cruise

Pleasure cruises on Loch Maree, operated by the steamer *Mabel*, ended when the Board of Trade refused to renew her safety certificate in the autumn of 1911. *Mabel* had been sailing on the loch since 1883, owned initially by the proprietor of the Loch Maree Hotel, Mr Hornsby, who also owned the Gairloch Hotel. In 1887 David MacBrayne Ltd bought her, and provided two daily sailings between Kinlochewe and Tollie during each season. After 1911 *Mabel* rusted away on the shore for forty years. Between the wars, a local man operated pleasure trips in his boat *Barracuda*, but these ended with fuel rationing in 1939.

The last forced eviction in Wester Ross occurred in Torridon when a tenant at Annat was driven out by the Earl of Lovelace's factor. The roof of the house was set on fire to ensure he did not return. The unfortunate man died a few weeks later in Shieldaig Poorhouse. *This incident was recalled in the superb book* 'Old Torridon' *by Murdoch Macdonald.*

John Macrae-Gilstrap bought the ruins of Eilean Donan Castle.

1914

Aultbea's United Free Church was built. It became disused after 1929 when the United Free Church merged with the Church of Scotland.

The last copper mine at Kishorn closed for good, after being sporadically worked for some years. Traces of the mine could still be seen years later above Rassal Ashwood, east of the road at Tornapress.

Inverewe House burnt down. Osgood Mackenzie moved to his other nearby property, Tournaig House.

Elsewhere, a number of land raids were carried out by landless cottars.

The Day War Broke Out: 4th August 1914

***Lady Fowler recalls a fateful day in* Records of the Men of Lochbroom**

It was probably with no more than an apathetic interest that anyone in Lochbroom had read, in those wondrous summer days of 1914, of the unrest in some of the states of Central Europe, which had been accentuated on June 28th by the assassination at Sarajevo of the heir-apparent to the throne of Austria and his wife.

Certainly it was with an almost amazed incredulity that I received from my eldest son,* at that time adjutant of the County Territorial Battalion, 4th Seaforths, the confidential information that a European war was believed to be imminent, and that every preparation was being made for the war organisation in Ross-shire to spring into activity on the first word of intimation received from headquarters. My son was at that time sleeping by the telephone in his office at Dingwall, so as not to miss the first word of instruction.

> ***A whisper reached us... the Government have begun to buy horses. Words of grave portent, as always indicating the imminence of war.***

In a few days it became apparent to the whole country that the question of 'war versus peace' was an acute one, and that almost any moment might bring the grave proclamation. But for a while no message came to relieve the suspense.

A whisper reached us: 'the government have begun to buy horses.' Words of grave portent, as always indicating the imminence of war. Then came the information: 'An order has been received in Dingwall from the government for fifty miles of barbed wire.' And finally, about half past nine on the evening of August 4th, when we were gathered in the drawing-room at Inverbroom with windows open and blinds up, watching the last glow fading in the western sky, and the shadows of night were beginning to fall around us, my daughter sprang to her feet, exclaiming that she had caught a glimpse in the garden of a man in motor-cyclist's dress.

A few moments later he was delivering to her the expected message from her brother, and quickly were the necessary papers filled in, acknowledging receipt of the order to mobilise. Entries in mobilisation forms were rapidly completed in accordance with instructions previously given by my son.

The motor-cyclist despatch rider, Councillor John Mackay, at once continued his 47 mile ride from Dingwall to Ullapool, not pausing to accept hospitality. Our young relative, Daniel Bayley, later a gallant officer of the Royal Artillery, mounted his bicycle and vanished into the darkness to deliver the necessary intimations of mobilisation to the various lads of the Territorial Force resident on the estate of Braemore. Thus did the Fiery Cross come to Lochbroom.

**Lady Fowler's sons John and Alan were killed in action within a year* (see next page)

The First World War claimed the lives of more than 200 men from Wester Ross and South-West Ross: an unthinkable and tragic loss for an area whose small population of 12,000 had already been falling before the war.

1914-18

1914

When war was declared on 4th August 1914, many men in Wester Ross were already training with local Territorial Army companies. Having signed up for five years, all could expect to be called up.

Within two weeks, 340 men from Wester Ross had left Dingwall for the south by train. 265 belonged to local companies of the **4th Battalion Seaforth Highlanders** - 135 men from Gairloch parish with 'D' company, 130 men from Lochbroom with 'E' company. Their war would be fought in France and Belgium. (Six other companies in the 4th Seaforths were based in Easter Ross.)

75 men from Lochcarron, Applecross and Lochalsh, already serving as territorials with the **Ross Mountain Battery**, left from Dingwall on 16th August - two days after the 4th Seaforths. Their war would be in Greece, Turkey and the Balkans.

Men from South-West Ross who already trained with 'E' squadron of the **2nd Lovat Scouts** based at Kyle, would go to the Balkans, Middle East and ultimately France in their specialist role of observers and snipers. The Lovat Scouts also had recruits among stalkers and shepherds from Gairloch and Lochbroom.

Other men joined regiments with no local territorial connection. The Cameron Highlanders were a popular choice: they formed part of the same Infantry Brigade as the Seaforths, with an HQ in Inverness. Many men also served in the navy.

In September 1914, the 2/4th Battalion of the Seaforth Highlanders was formed to provide reinforcements; men already posted became known as the 1/4th. Later a 3/4th was also formed. In November the 1/4th Seaforths were one of the first territorial battalions to leave Britain for France. Each division reaching France was numbered from 42 to 56, and the Highland Territorial Division, to which the 4th Seaforths had belonged before the war and which they re-joined in 1916, became the 51st - a number which would become a symbol of distinction.

1915

On 10-11th March at **Neuve Chapelle**, the 4th Battalion Seaforth Highlanders faced their first major action and suffered the loss of 168 men. In May, during an unsuccessful attack on **Aubers Ridge**, over 200 losses were sustained.

Major John Mackenzie VC, of Lochluichart, who in 1914 had joined the Bedfordshire regiment from the Royal Scots, was killed in action on 17th May. Sir John Fowler, Captain with the 2nd Seaforths, was killed in June just weeks after his younger brother Alan had fallen in action with the Cameron Highlanders.

In May the Ross Mountain Battery, who had been sent east to take part in the **Gallipoli** landings, suffered their first losses, including two men from Wester Ross: Gunner D.Mackenzie of Carndhu by Dornie, and Gunner J.Macrae, Kishorn.

In September and October, the 4th Seaforths were involved in the Battle of **Loos**, though because the battalion had been severely depleted they did not actually fight - a unit of 100 men being assigned to protect cylinders of poison gas.

The effect of reports of deaths on the community at home in Wester Ross can hardly be imagined. Meanwhile prisoner-of-war camps were set up, including one at Braemore, where German POWs were given work felling timber. Kyle began to play a key role in the movement of equipment and mines by rail to Dalmore and Invergordon naval bases.

1916

From January 1916 until the end of the war, the 4th Battalion Seaforth Highlanders fought as part of the 51st (Highland) Division (154th Brigade). The battalion were involved in the Battle of the **Somme** between July and November.

At home, the whole area north of the Great Glen, including Wester Ross, was declared a special military area in July. Only holders of permits could travel.

1917

At **Arras** in April, the 1/4th Seaforths were in the first line of the 51st Highland Division as it attacked successfully, but the battalion suffered over 200 casualties.

Between June and September, at the **3rd Battle of Ypres**, the 4th Seaforths encountered poison gas for the first time. Then at **Cambrai** in November, the battalion took part in the first-ever major tank battle. The offensive was a relative success but cost the battalion 300 men.

At home the Ministry of Agriculture, worried about the need for food, ordered 10,000 acres of land to be broken up for sowing. Legislation was passed to allow the compulsory purchase of land for servicemen after the war.

1918

The 4th Seaforths were one of many regiments to face a huge German onslaught during the spring. In October, the battalion took part in a final Allied attack, advancing from Cambrai to Valenciennes, in the course of which they suffered 300 losses.

The armistice bringing the war to an end was signed on 11th November.

1919

On New Year's Day, the ship *Iolaire* sank while sailing from Kyle to Stornoway, with the loss of 250 men (75 survived). All victims were naval ratings returning from war.The ship hit rocks yards off Lewis.

Throughout 1919, servicemen returned home to Wester Ross. Some made their own way back after being demobilised in England, others came as a unit. In April, men still serving with the Ross Mountain Battery were welcomed to Dingwall. They had finished their war in Salonica.

Peace Sunday was celebrated in churches on 6th July, Peace Day on the 19th. In August, a Great Victory Joint Show was held at Dingwall. Men of the 4th Seaforths attended a reception at Brahan Castle. In October, the last 58 men still serving with the battalion returned to Ross-shire as a unit.

An area of deer forest in Glenshiel was bought under the Defence of the Realm Act 1917, to be given to ex-servicemen.

Education Authorities took over from School Boards. The Ross-shire authority was elected in June. The Forestry Commission was established; by 1921 it had purchased large areas of Wester Ross for planting. The Ministry of Transport and Ministry of Health were set up; a Medical Inspector appointed for Ross-shire.

Every war memorial tells the same tragic story, though each seems to highlight something unique. Nine men from the small population around Kinlochewe were killed, five with the Seaforths.

The Kinlochewe memorial also pays tribute to two men who died from the effects of wounds long after the war ended. Sergeant J.MacLennan, DCM, died in 1921 and Sergeant M.Macrae, DCM, in 1930.

RECORDS OF SACRIFICE

The Lochalsh memorial records 62 men killed including 15 Seaforth Highlanders, eight Camerons and 17 men who had emigrated and fought with New Zealand, Australian or Canadian forces.

The war memorial at Lochcarron lists the names of 30 men who died.

The Garve memorial commemorates 33 men, 13 with the Seaforths. Two sons of the proprietor of Strathvaich died - war had no respect for rank or privilege. 14 men from around Little Loch Broom died, six with the Seaforths. Three were from Scoraig.

John Mackenzie VC lies buried in Plot 8, Row J, Grave 10, of the Guards Cemetery at Windy Corner, near Cuinchy in France.

A District's Losses: Aultbea

Seaforths	***Scots Guards***
Pte. R.Mackenzie	**Gdsmn. W.MacIver**
Cpl. K.Mackenzie	***Canadians***
Pte. M.Mackenzie	**Pte. K.Mackenzie**
Pte. J.Mackenzie	**Lieut. H.Mackenzie**
L-Cpl. H.Mackenzie	***Australians***
Pte. J.MacLean	**Sgt. D.Macleod**
Pte. C.Macrae	***NZEF***
Pte. R.Tulloch	**Pte. J.Mackenzie**
Pte. D.Macleod	***NZD***
Pte. D.Maclennan	**Pte. R.Beaton**
Camerons	***RFA***
Capt. K.MacIver	**Fr.Sgt. A.Campbell**
Lieut. D.MacIver	**Gnr. A.Mackenzie**
Sgt. J.Macleod	***RND***
Gordons	**A.B. Z.Maclennan**
Pte. R.Maclennan	***Royal Naval Reserve***
Pte. A.Mackenzie	**Stkr. A.Macleod**
Scots Horse	**A.B. J.MacLean**
L-Cpl. J.Maclennan	**A.B. H.May**
Capt. A.Murray	**A.B. D.MacIver**
Scots Rifles	**A.B. A.Urquhart**
Piper J.MacIver	**Smn. M.Maclennan**
Pte. J.Maclennan	*(34 men killed)*

4th Battalion, Seaforth Highlanders: Local Men Lost

	Born in	*Killed*		*Born in*	*Killed*
Murdo Campbell	Lochbroom	1915	Hector Bain	Gairloch	1917
Murdo MacDonald	Gairloch	1915	John Fraser	Gairloch	1917
Roderick MacDonald	Applecross	1915	Edward Laurie	Gairloch	1917
Donald MacIver	Gairloch	1915	Alexander Mackenzie	Gairloch	1917
Finlay MacIver	Gairloch	1915	Alexander Mackenzie	Applecross	1917
Donald MacKay	Lochluichart	1915	William MacDonald	Lochalsh	1917
Alexander MacLean	Gairloch	1915	Alexander McGregor	Lochbroom	1917
Kenneth MacLean	Lochbroom	1915	Murdo Mackenzie	Lochbroom	1917
Duncan MacLean	Lochbroom	1915	John Mackenzie	Gairloch	1917
Kenneth Mackenzie	Lochbroom	1915	John Mackenzie	Lochcarron	1917
Alexander Mackenzie	Gairloch	1915	Kenneth Mackenzie	Lochbroom	1917
Duncan Mackenzie	Lochcarron	1915	Angus Mackenzie	Gairloch	1917
Donald Morrison	Lochcarron	1915	Norman MacLean	Lochbroom	1917
William Ross	Gairloch	1915	Donald MacLennan	Lochbroom	1917
Simon Urquhart	Lochbroom	1915	John Miller	Gairloch	1917
Hector MacLennan	Gairloch	1915	Duncan MacLeod	Gairloch	1917
Alexander MacLennan	Gairloch	1915	Kenneth MacKenzie	Gairloch	1918
Hugh MacLeod	Lochbroom	1916	Donald Campbell	Lochbroom	1918
Murdo MacLeod	Lochbroom	1916	Duncan Gordon	Gairloch	1918
Donald Matheson	Lochalsh	1916	Alexander MacAulay	Lochalsh	1918

Alexander Macrae from Lochbroom died of wounds on Armistice Day 1918

(Source: Seaforth Highlanders Records. Note: list excludes local men not born in the area)

Story of the 2nd & 4th Seaforths

Over the years many men from Wester Ross have served with the Seaforth Highlanders, most in either the 2nd battalion (regular) or the 4th (territorial). The regiment evolved as follows:

1778: The 7th Earl of Seaforth raised the *78th Regiment of (Highland) Foot.*

1786: Re-numbered as *72nd (Highland) Regiment of Foot.*

1793: Col. F.Humberston Mackenzie of Brahan raised a new regiment, the *78th Highland Regiment of Foot.*

1794: Second battalion of the 78th raised, known as the *Ross-shire Buffs.*

1796: The 78th battalions amalgamated.

1804: 2nd battalion of the 78th re-raised.

1809: 72nd re-named *72nd Regiment of Foot.*

1816: Both 78th battalions again amalgamated, as the *78th Highlanders (Ross-shire Buffs).*

1824: 72nd re-named *72nd (Duke of Albany's Own) Highlanders.*

1881: The 72nd and 78th regiments amalgamated as the Seaforth Highlanders, with the former 78th Highlanders (Ross-shire Buffs) becoming the *2nd Battalion.* The Highland Rifle Militia became the 3rd (Militia) Battalion. A designated 'territorial area' - the Northern Highlands - was given to the Seaforths, and three volunteer battalions in that area, including the *1st Ross-shire (Ross Highland) Rifle Volunteers*, were now affiliated.

1908: The Ross-shire Rifle Volunteers were re-designated as the *4th Battalion of the Seaforth Highlanders.*

1920: Territorial Army re-formed.

1921: 4th & 5th Seaforths amalgamated as the '4/5th Battalion'.

1939: 4th & 5th Battalions re-formed.

27 Victoria Crosses have been awarded to the regiment. During the First World War, over 8,000 Seaforth Highlanders were killed.

John Mackenzie VC (from an old image held at Fort George)

An Inspector Calls

Writing in the 1920s, John Wilson recalled a long and stimulating career travelling the Highlands as an Inspector of Schools.

A visit by an Inspector was an occasion for great trepidation among teachers and school board members. On his examination and subsequent report, along with attendance and discipline records, depended the level of grant which the school received the following year.

A member of the Board, which usually comprised local lairds, ministers and other 'worthies', would accommodate the Inspector during his visit. Wilson appreciated such hospitality. Though strict about his duties, he was also partial to a good dram.

If the examination was protracted, a pause was deemed necessary to let the examinees get a breathing space and much needed 'piece'. And what was more natural than that the Inspector should go into the schoolhouse for a sip of something to sustain him for the remainder of the examination. This completed, an adjournment was as a rule made to the teacher's house or the manse for lunch. Here the usual appetiser was proffered. More liquor was on the table to wash down the roast beef and greens; and it would have been insulting to his host if the Inspector left without a deoch-an-doruis...

This was in Wilson's earlier career, and times changed.

Today the Inspector motors from school to school practically unrecognised by the general public.

A Century of Books

1900 Robert Bain: ***History of the Ancient Province of Ross***
1905 W.J.Watson: ***Place Names of Ross and Cromarty***
1920 Alexander Polson: ***Gairloch***
1921 Osgood Mackenzie: ***A Hundred Years in the Highlands*** *(his life at Inverewe)*. Later books on Inverewe Gardens were:
Dawn MacLeod: ***Oasis of the North***
May Cowan: ***Inverewe: Garden in the North-West Highlands***
1922 Alice Fowler: ***Records of the Men of Lochbroom***
1928 John Wilson: ***Tales and Travels of a School Inspector***
1935 Seton Gordon: ***Highways and Byways in the West Highlands***
1940 Frank Fraser Darling: ***Island Years***; then (1944) ***Island Farm***
Later works: ***West Highland Survey***; ***Highlands and Islands***
1946 Duncan Macpherson: ***Gateway to Skye***
Later works: (1950) ***Lure of the West;*** (1964) ***Where I Belong***
1948 Brenda Macrow: ***Kintail Scrapbook***; (1953) ***Torridon Highlands***
1960 Gavin Maxwell: ***Ring of Bright Water*** Sequels:
(1963) ***The Rocks Remain***; (1968) ***Raven Seek Thy Brother***
1975 Lea MacNally: ***Year of the Red Deer*** Later works included:
(1993) ***Torridon, Life and Wildlife in the Scottish Highlands***
1976 James Hunter: ***The Making of the Crofting Community***
Later works included: (1991) ***The Claim of Crofting***
1977 Gairloch Heritage Museum: ***Gairloch & Guide to Loch Maree*** *(reprint of J.H.Dixon's late 19th century classic)*
1978 Jean Dunlop: ***The British Fisheries Society 1786-1893***
1979 Earl of Cromartie: ***Cromartie - A Highland History*** *(the Cromartie lands included Coigach and Dundonnell)*
1983 Iain Thomson: ***Isolation Shepherd*** *(life by Loch Monar)*
1987 ***Third Statistical Account for Scotland, Ross & Cromarty***
1988 Christina Byam Shaw: ***Pigeonholes of Memory*: Life and Times of Dr John Mackenzie 1803-86** *(life in Gairloch)*
1988 R.Mackenzie (ed J.Michael): ***Tales and Legends of Lochbroom***
1989 E.Richards, M.Clough: ***Cromartie: Highland Life 1650-1914***
1989 Ian Sykes (ed.): ***Duncraig Castle, Plockton***
1991 A.M.G.Ball: ***A Pinch of Salt*** *(people and places in Lochcarron, South-West Ross and Skye)*
1992 Kenneth MacLennan: ***Memories of Strathvaich***
1994 Tom MacIver: ***Croft Remote*** *(a childhood in Coigach)*
1994 John Baldwin (ed): ***Peoples & Settlement in North-West Ross***
1996 Steve Chadwick: ***Loch Ewe During World War Two***
1997 Murdoch Macdonald: ***Old Torridon***
1998 Roger Miket: ***Glenelg, Kintail and Lochalsh***
1999 C.J.Uncles: ***Old Ways through Wester Ross*** *(period photos)*
2000 Kenneth C.Mackenzie: ***The River Ewe***
2000 Smithy Heritage Centre: ***Bygone Years*** *(local photos and text)*

Torridon and Whisky

There were many lighter moments in John Wilson's career. While staying at Torridon House with the laird Duncan Darroch, he was asked by Mrs Darroch if he would like a day's fishing. It was pouring rain, so he declined. But she had a large house-party to feed and insisted. A ghillie, Angus, was found. The two men had a long day and came back soaked and in need of refreshment.

Although I knew quite well that my host abhorred spirituous liquor, I ventured to ask Angus where a 'drop' might be obtained. After some misgiving, he led me to the cottage of an old woman, to whom he explained our plight in most forceful Gaelic.

They were given their whisky.

My small share I liberally diluted with water, but adhering to the custom of his ancestors, Angus gulped down a half cupful of the vile, fiery liquid with the usual announcement 'I will be taking the water afterwards'. Like his forebears, he never did.

On another occasion, Wilson inspected Alligin School, with Mr Darroch present in the schoolroom.

Forgetful for the moment that the natives of Alligin were notorious smugglers, I was questioning the pupils on the nature of smuggling, when smiles took the place of answers. The pupils whose relatives had to do with it blushed scarlet, and no doubt the laird, though he never let on, noted this.

Keeping Order

Many teachers taught alone, in smaller schools, and a few found it difficult to keep discipline.

When the gentle young female who taught a small school on the shore of a loch in Wester Ross demitted office, parents sent a deputation to urge on the School Board that better discipline would be maintained, and consequently better results secured, were a man appointed to fill the vacancy. The Board, however, refused to accede, chiefly because they knew that the salary paid to a female would be quite inadequate for the services of a male teacher.

Instead, the board transferred a woman teacher from another school, 'six feet high with shoulders half as broad'. There were no complaints!

Tales & Travels of a School Inspector was published in 1928 and re-printed by Acair in 1998.

The Twenties and Thirties

The two decades between the world wars saw another sharp decline in the population of Wester Ross, with many young people moving to the cities or overseas in search of better prospects.

For others who remained, life was hard. Many widows had to struggle to bring up families alone after the war. For some men, wounded in the trenches, life was never the same again. Reports of untimely deaths were common into the 1930s. The market for herring collapsed in the early 1920s, when important export markets in Germany and Russia were lost. The price of cattle, sheep and wool also collapsed at this time. Rationing continued into the 1920s.

Meanwhile communities raised funds to build memorials.

Under the 1919 Land Settlement (Scotland) Act, it was intended that land should be made available to ex-servicemen, and Leacachan farm in Glenshiel was broken up to form a sheep stock club. But progress was patchy - there were more land raids in the islands in protest.

Life was hard, even before the Depression of the early 1930s. But there was some material progress: electric lighting at Ullapool, for example, and a water supply at Dornie. Perhaps more importantly, though, family and community life held up strong, as Barbara MacLennan's story of her childhood and youth illustrates.

Diary of a Year

1920

No Escape from War

Inmates of the quiet little township of Achduart, situated four miles east of Achiltibuie Hotel, were rudely awakened in the early hours of last Sunday morning by a loud report, the result of an explosion from a live mine on the seashore, about half a mile to the west of the village.

On Saturday evening, Mr Roderick Macrae, who resides in the vicinity, while on his way home, noticed the mine on the shore, and thinking that it had already exploded and that therefore all danger was passed, went to the beach and fastened the mine to a rock, leaving it there. As the tide flowed in, it lifted the mine, and coming in contact with the rocks it exploded, the report of the explosion being heard for miles around. Huge boulders were blown up in all directions, while a portion of the heather on the hillside was burned through getting ignited by sparks from the mine.

Fishermen living on Tanera Mor have moored another live mine in the channel dividing the island from Tanera Beag.

Ross-shire Journal, 12th March

Tragic Accident

Two fishermen belonging to Tanera Mor, James Campbell and Dougal Mathieson, drowned while lobster fishing in May - a terrible blow to a fragile island population.

District Nurse Appointed

Lochcarron Nursing Association was formed at a meeting where it was also agreed to apppoint a District Nurse. Lady Murray of Lochcarron Estate was thanked for personally funding local nursing care during recent years.

Life Goes On

Annual shows which had been suspended since 1914 were held again as people made an effort to return to a semblance of normality *(see over)*.

Harnessing Nature

The possibility of providing hydro-electric power in Kintail was discussed by Alexander Edward, the local landowner, who criticised a lack of will among public authorities for the absence of schemes in the West Highlands to date. Only private enterprise, he believed, would ensure action and he described his plans for supplying electricity to local cottages.

I am at the present time arranging to heat and light the crofters' and cottars' houses on my estate of Kintail from the water power derived from some of the small streams rushing down the side of one of the Five Sisters.

When I get my scheme completed, the good housewives of Kintail will be perfectly independent of miners' strikes, both in coal and shale, and I reckon that they will have their heat and light at less than one half of what they are paying now.

Jobs Vacant: 1920

After the war, much had changed but the old social order remained. There were long lists of 'servants wanted' adverts in the press each week. This is from the *Ross-shire Journal*, January 1920.

Wanted, upper and under housemaids, country mansion. Permanent. Small family, seven servants.

Of 24 vacancies in that issue, 19 were for domestic staff. Wealthy employers were often outnumbered by their servants:

Can any lady recommend a cook for a family of four (six maids kept) near London, returning to Scotland next spring. Wages £50.

Some job descriptions could only have belonged to the Highlands. The Head Stalker on Drumrunie Estate looked for

a ghillie, able to work dogs, good boatman essential. Piper preferred. Wages £3 per week.

* * *

Forestry provided new opportunities for employment. Lord Lovat, a key figure in the establishment of the Forestry Commission in 1919, opened a school of forestry at Beaufort Castle.

Military service was another option, although probably not holding much appeal to men who had been in the war.

Wanted. A few smart men between the ages of 18 and 25 for the county regiment, the Seaforth Highlanders. Apply to Recruiting Officer, Dingwall.

The lure of a better life abroad may have been too great for some who read adverts like this:

Ontario wants farm workers and domestic servants. Splendid opportunities await industrious, ambitious workers in Canada's leading agricultural and industrial province.

Left: Eilean Donan Castle was re-built between 1913 and 1932
Centre: Aultbea and Loch Ewe
Bottom: Nostie Post Office: humble but useful to its community, and sadly now closed

C.Pashley

C.Pashley

Plockton, with Duncraig Castle in the background

Much of the text in this book is taken up with the problem of transport in Wester Ross during the 20th century - and this picture illustrates the sort of difficulties travellers could face. The Bealach na Ba is still an impressive route, but before it was upgraded,and before the days of snowploughs, it could be impassable for weeks at a time. The residents of Applecross largely depended on boats for access and for supplies.

C.Pashley

Painful Reminder

When minesweeper HMS *Burslem* was in port at Kyle, a correspondent of the *Ross-shire Journal* commented: *The presence of the boys in blue is a vivid reminder of the nightmare of war when sailors and soldiers in the streets far outnumbered the civilian population.*

Outdoor Service

An outdoor Communion service was held at Gairloch for the first time since the war. The service, at the traditional site of *Leapadh-na-ba-bhaine* ('the bed of the white cow') was conducted in July by Rev. Mackinnon, the Free Church minister. A stalwart of the anti-Union movement, he was minister at Gairloch from 1894 until his death in 1925.

Lochcarron Golf Course

Mr Taylor, the new proprietor of Tullich Estate, offered Lochcarron Golf Club land to extend their course to 18 holes. The offer was declined, however, as the club wished to concentrate efforts meantime on improving the nine-hole course.

A smallpox outbreak on the Black Isle in September caused alarm throughout the Highlands. Voluntary vaccinations were encouraged.

1920 (continued)

War Memorial Unveiled

One of the first war memorials in Wester Ross was erected by Sir Kenneth and Lady Marjory Mackenzie at the Crask, Gairloch. The names of 63 dead from their own estate, including their son Lieutenant Roderick Mackenzie of the Black Watch, were inscribed on the handsome freestone monument, a copy of the ancient cross at Scone Palace.

Kinlochewe Church of Scotland was opened *(see 2000).*

Paying the Rates

Until 1930, ratepayers were assessed each year by their parish council for payment of five different rates: *education, burial, registration, poor* and *special rates.* In August 1920, Lochbroom Parish Council reported that there would have to be an increase in the poor rate, through which poor relief and the poorhouse were funded. However, in compensation, there would be a reduction in other rates, with the effect that the total levy on parish ratepayers would in fact be approximately 3d per pound less than in 1919.

Cattle Shows

Lochcarron Cattle Show was held for the first time in August. There were 99 entries for cattle, 60 for sheep and 20 in the horse section. Among prize-winners were local club farms of Coulags, Arinackaig, and Achintee. Club farms were co-operative ventures, established all over the Highlands after the war, with members pooling resources. Several still exist today, though with fewer members. Lochbroom Cattle Show was also held at Dundonnell - for the third time, but the first since the war. Crofters decided to continue the pre-war plan of alternating venues, with the next two years' shows at Coigach and Ullapool.

Honeymooning

Miss Urquhart, Melvaig, and Mr Hall, Rubha Reidh Lighthouse married at the Free Church, Gairloch in August, with a reception afterwards at the Gairloch Hotel. The *Ross-shire Journal* reported: *After the function the happy couple motored to Londubh, where the honeymoon will be spent amidst the lovely scenery of Loch Maree and Poolewe.* This trip involved a distance of less than twenty miles from home: quite an adventure, however, in those days, and with the novelty of hiring a car.

New Boat for Food Supply Service

In May the Ministry of Food chartered a new steamer, *Rosedale,* to take over from the *Bessie* on a regular supply service between Mallaig, Kyle, Skye and Wester Ross. Aultbea was the boat's northernmost port of call. The service distributed goods brought to Mallaig by train.

"Freight charges rail-cum-drifter will not be materially higher than by direct steamers from Glasgow", the ministry stated. From June, *Rosedale* sailed from Mallaig every fortnight, calling at **Armadale, Isle Ornsay, Glenelg, Kyle, Portree, Staffin, Aultbea**, **Inverasdale**, **Badachro**, **Gairloch**, **Diabaig**, **Alligin**, **Torridon**, **Shieldaig** and **Fearnbeg**, returning to Kyle every second Wednesday, and Mallaig on Thursday to connect with the afternoon train.

From the Ross-shire Journal, *December*

Peats have been supplied to Laide School at 10d a creel.

Road and Rail News

A new road to Port Henderson was approved by the Gairloch District Committee of the County Council. In order to ensure that the road was built, and to bring down its cost by a quarter, men of the local community offered their services in free labour.

* * *

The need for a road along the west shore of Loch Broom to Loggie was discussed by the Lochbroom District Committee. Unfortunately Loggie was to remain roadless for many years yet.

* * *

Rail to Ullapool?

Efforts were made during 1920 to revive interest in building a railway from Garve to Ullapool. The first promoters of such a project had secured an Act of Parliament for it in 1890, with the Highland Railway Company promising to operate the line. But the plan fell through when the Highland Railway decided instead to concentrate on an extension from Stromeferry to Kyle, for which they obtained an Act in 1894.

The war had stopped some planned new railways in their tracks. The proposed Dingwall & Cromarty Railway had been three-quarters built by 1914, but it never opened. The track was removed for use in the war effort.

* * *

During 1920, the future of the railway network was under discussion. The Minister of Transport decided to create four groups of railways from the dozens of existing private companies.

* * *

Tractors for Sale

By 1920 an extensive range of cars, motor-cycles and tractors was available for sale or for hire. The County Garage, Dingwall, described their latest tractor: *The Fordson Tractor undertakes to haul by mechanical power everything driven during harvest on the farm by horses. The tractor starts on petrol and runs on paraffin. 22hp. 3-speed & reverse. Price at works £260.*

Land Raided on Lewis

Land raiders on Lewis agreed to evacuate farms which they had seized at Back and Coll, to allow the Government and Board of Agriculture to address the whole issue of returning land seized during the Clearances to crofting.

Good Fishing

Fishing at Plockton on 3rd June, three visitors who were staying at the local hotel had a good day, landing four whiting, nine cod - and 115 haddock.

Loch Maree Timber Trade

A ship from the Isle of Man sailed from Poolewe in August with a load of timber cut from forests around Loch Maree. In September another boat sailed with a final load of the season, bound for Troon.

New Club Room

Major C.J.Murray of Lochcarron Estate presented the community with a club and reading-room, located in the upper flat of a reconstructed house adjoining the Drill Hall.

The General Stores
More than a Shop

Within every community were places such as the smithy, mill or general stores which acted as a sort of hub for the life of the district. Alistair MacLean recalled how, in Torridon, the men of the district would meet in the general merchant's shop at Annat of an evening to smoke and put the world to rights.

Beauty's Stores, Lochcarron, was an example of a business that kept village life going in diverse ways. John Mackenzie, known from childhood as 'Beauty' - his brother Jimmy was 'Bonny' - started business by setting up a bakehouse and baker's shop in the village, adding the Supply Stores later. The retail side was expanded until it sold ironmongery, clothing, footwear, bicycles, crockery, and household furnishings. Goods were brought in by puffer.

But John did not stop there. A taxi service and van round were started. Coal was delivered by lorry, a petrol station and garage were opened. John built a jetty and hired a boat. He also built the electric generating plant known as the power house. A biscuit known as Beauty's Wine was made at the bakehouse, and distributed throughout the Highlands.

The business was sold in the 1920s.

A Great Storm

On 15th November 1920 a severe storm lashed Wester Ross, washing away the railway line in two places near Attadale and preventing trains from running for 24 hours.

Torridon also suffered.

The footbridge over the Balgy River was blown away by the gale and all communication by land between Shieldaig and Torridon absolutely cut off. Before a new bridge can be erected, much public inconvenience must result.

The parish doctor lives at Torridon, and his patients at Shieldaig cannot receive a medical attendance except by hiring a motor-boat to convey the doctor by sea. The three ministers reside at Shieldaig, and they too are cut off from their people at Torridon.

Ross-shire Journal, 26th November

The incident came at a time when local ratepayers had been urging the county Roads Board to construct a road between Torridon and Shieldaig. But local landowners opposed the idea and it was not until 1963 that a proper road was built.

To Drink or Not

The Temperance movement was still powerful in 1920. The newly created Scottish Board of Liquor Control had been given powers to restrict licensing as it saw fit. In the autumn, a vote was held in all parts of Scotland (but not in England), on three possible options for future licensing:

a) total prohibition on alcohol sales except in hotels and restaurants

b) the withdrawal of a quarter of existing licences

c) no change

Gairloch for prohibition

With few exceptions across the country, the vote went in favour of 'no change'. One exception, however, was the parish of Gairloch, where 124 people voted in favour of prohibition, 26 voted to reduce the number of licences by a quarter, and 123 voted for 'no change'. However, rules laid down that more than 35% of the electorate must have voted, and this had not been achieved. So there was no change - and six licensees in the parish could breathe again!

Prohibition was declared in the United States in 1920.

Food Rationing

Throughout 1920 the District Food Officer for Ross-shire issued regular bulletins on changes in allowances. In July, an extra 1.5 pounds of sugar per person, for use in making jam, was made available at a reduced price.

Crofting and Farming

During 1920 there was concern about prospects for those crofters who had recently bought their croft-house and improved it, and who were now faced with a higher valuation being placed on the property - and hence having to pay rates which were higher than their previous rent. This is a debate which has recurred since, especially after legislation in the 1970s made it possible to purchase an entire croft.

* * *

For those with the capital to farm rather than croft in 1920, a typical price for a farm of about 1000 acres, with house and other buildings, was between £1000 and £2000 (a lot of money). In January, farm labourers in Ross-shire demanded a 48-hour week and a minimum wage of £3 per week.

* * *

1920 saw the last-ever cattle-drove in Scotland, from Argyll to the market at Stirling. It was the end of an era for the cattle trade, once the mainstay of Wester Ross.

Showing Tonight

The **Picture House** in Dingwall was the nearest cinema to Wester Ross in 1920. Transport being what it was, it was not practical for most people to go to see a film - but for those who could, *Less than Kin* starring Wallace Reid, was showing in early January, and the following week, the Charlie Chaplin film *Tillie's Punctured Romance*. These movies were, of course, silent. There were shows every evening except Sunday, and on Saturday afternoon. Adults paid 1s.3d. or 9d., children 5d.

The Twenties

1921

War memorials were unveiled at Lochcarron and Lochalsh.

The Forestry Commission purchased land for afforestation at Strome, and in subsequent years other substantial acreages at Craig, Achnashellach, Inverinate, Ratagan and Inverlael.

Prime Minister Mr Lloyd-George visited Gairloch in September.

War memorials at Aultbea and Poolewe were unveiled.

In August, a tragic incident claimed eight lives and made headline news. The victims all died from food-poisoning after eating sandwiches prepared in the kitchen at the Loch Maree Hotel. Two were local ghillies, the others were guests staying at the hotel. They had been out on a shooting trip and eaten potted duck. An inquiry later identified botulism as the cause of death.

Ullapool Lights Up

Electric light was provided for the first time in Ullapool in November. A generating station known as the 'power house' was built on land where Mackay's Garage later stood, on the present-day Latheron Lane. The scheme was funded by a donation of £500 from James Stewart, agent for the National Bank, in memory of his uncle, and a connection was offered free of charge to local businesses.

1923

A war memorial for townships round Little Loch Broom was unveiled.

The Highland Railway Company was absorbed into a new grouping of companies, the London Midland & Scottish Railway, better known in due course as the LMS.

Pioneering Trust

Across the Minch Lord Leverhulme, frustrated in his plans to promote commercial and industrial ventures on Lewis, turned to Harris instead but before quitting Lewis offered his lands to the local parish councils. The Stornoway councillors accepted his offer of land in and around the town and formed the Stornoway Trust to manage it. In doing so they set an example for communities who would try to buy land in the 1990s.

A Colourful Life

Osgood Mackenzie, 1842-1922

Osgood Mackenzie is remembered as the creator of Inverewe Gardens but he was also the author of a fascinating memoir, *A Hundred Years in the Highlands*. His life spanned remarkable changes. As a small boy in the 1840s, he cut the first turf on the 'Destitution Road' along Loch Maree, so named because its purpose was to provide work and wages for those suffering in the wake of the potato famine. In later life he drove his motor-car along that same road.

Mackenzie recalled how, during his childhood in Gairloch, the lighting in most houses was provided by firelight or using oil from fish, quite a contrast from the electric light which was provided in Ullapool in the last year of his life *(see above)*.

The black houses depended for light chiefly on the roaring fires in the centre of the room, with perhaps an old creel or barrel stuck in the roof to let out the smoke. For use in very exceptional cases the people had tiny tin lamps, made by the tinkers and fed with oil made out of the livers of fish which were allowed to get rotten before they were boiled down.

But the main lighting at night was done by having a big heap of carefully prepared bog-fir splinters full of resin all ready in a corner. A small boy or girl did nothing else but keep these burning during the evening, so that the women could see to card and spin and the men to make their herring-nets by hand.

Osgood Mackenzie's passions throughout his life, apart from the creation of his garden at Inverewe, were shooting and egg-collecting.

Few men have done more shooting in the course of their lives than I have. Vermin consisted of all kinds of beasts and birds, a good many of which are now extinct.

His account does at least give the reader an appreciation of why the conservation movement started in the 20th century!

The End of the Strath Mill

Death of the Colonel

Since the early 17th century a mill had been in operation in the centre of Strath, Gairloch, although the building itself had been re-constructed several times. It was served by water from the Abhainn Bail a' Ghobhainn, which runs through the village. The life and times of the mill were later recalled by Donald Macintyre.

The last of the millers, Roderick Forbes, was known as 'the Colonel' on account of his somewhat pompous manner and posh accent. As he was also a church elder, he was undoubtedly one of the village 'heavies'.

Anyone with a moment or two to spare could drop into the boatyard, the blacksmith, the tailor, the bakery or any one of the local shops for a bit of crack, in the sense of passing the time of day. But the mill had an additional attraction - the kiln. The furnace-room, especially on a cold dark winter's night, provided a cosy haven, and the Colonel, who thus gained an army of unpaid stokers, was more than willing to allow the kiln to be used as the village meeting-place.

A sluice-gate at Mial allowed water into the mill-race.

The Colonel would walk up to open the gate (really a flat stone) in the upper dam, sit down, cut and rub up his black twist tobacco, light his pipe, and not till then, make his leisurely way back down to the mill. He still had ample time to prepare for milling before the rush of water!

Osgood Mackenzie recalled seeing boats arrive at the shore below Strath mill, carrying oats and bere in sheepskin bags "with a certain amount of wool still on their outsides to remind one of their origin". Sheepskins, he recalled, were also used for riddling meal; after being stretched, the skins were perforated with a red-hot needle.

During the 1914-18 war, work fell away at the Strath mill. No new apprentice had been trained by the time of Mr Forbes's death in 1922. The mill closed, and became derelict.

1924

War memorials were unveiled at Shieldaig and Lochluichart.

The Highland Home Industries Association staged their annual *Highland Village Industrial Exhibitions* during August and September. Various other highlights of the summer calendar included the *Garve Flower Show* in August and the *Black Isle Farmers' Society Show*, also in August and still a major event in the north today.

War memorials were unveiled at Ullapool and Plockton.

A water scheme was approved for Lochcarron at a cost of £800. But the community would have to wait some years yet for a satisfactory supply, one of the local ministers commenting in the 1950s that the village still depended on a few pumps for most of its water.

1926

Children of Achiltibuie and Achduart Schools were entertained to a Christmas treat in Achiltibuie Hotel by Mrs Cadbury (of the chocolate family), a regular visitor to Coigach, who provided a Christmas tree: reportedly the first in the district.

1927

The Tweed Mill at Braes, Ullapool, closed. The mill, set up in the 1890s by borders weavers, was reported to have had problems with new dyes fading.

> **Fed up with Officialdom**
>
> Red tape is nothing new, to judge by this letter to the *Ross-shire Journal* in the early 1920s.
>
> *It used to be said that one rifle bullet aimed along the High Street of a certain town would bring down at least half a dozen public officials. Today, rifles being more powerful and officials more numerous, the casualties would surely be greater.*

The End of the Sheila

The mail steamer *Sheila*, sailing from Kyle to Stornoway, was wrecked on New Year's Day off the Applecross coast near Cuaig, after being blown off course while trying to make her scheduled stop in Applecross Bay. The Harris mailboat *Plover* sailed from Kyle that afternoon in an attempt to rescue those on board, but darkness had fallen and it was not until Sunday 2nd that she was able to take off the 8 passengers and some of the crew along with the mails. *Sheila* was finally abandoned on the Monday.

The Ross-shire Electric Supply Co Ltd took over the Dingwall & Strathpeffer Electric Co Ltd and began construction of a hydro-electric scheme in Strathconon which involved a dam on Loch Luichart.

Duncan MacPherson published the first edition of his vest pocket guide to Lochalsh and Skye, which appeared annually until 1960. The chemist at Kyle since 1912, he also wrote three books and was a distinguished photographer.

A war memorial to men of clan Macrae was unveiled at Clachan Duich church.

Education Authority plans to cut staff at Ullapool Higher Grade School caused concern in the community, who feared the school was to be downgraded. Despite their fears - later proved correct - a substantial new school was built on Quay Street and opened in 1929.

Alexander Mackenzie, a stalker of Iron Lodge, one of the most remote houses in the area, retired after 31 years. As was often the way of things, he was succeeded by his son, who had grown up there.

1928

The Grampian Electricity Supply Company announced plans for a hydro-electric scheme in Glen Strathfarrar and Glen Affric. Meanwhile a temporary dam was washed away during the construction of Loch Luichart hydro-electric scheme.

> **Equality for Women**
>
> Women over 21 and women who were single finally won the right to vote in 1928. Previously only married women over 30 could vote.

In May the flagship of the British fleet, *HMS Hood*, visited Loch Kishorn.

David MacBrayne Ltd were unable to renew their contract to operate west coast mail steamer services because of a financial crisis. The Government invited tenders, but there were none until the LMS Railway Co and Coast Lines Ltd stepped in to re-constitute the firm as *David MacBrayne (1928) Ltd.* MacBrayne retired, ending a family involvement of 50 years.

A sub-branch of the Bank of Scotland was opened at Kinlochewe one day per week, staffed from the Gairloch branch.

Luichart Power Station was opened by the Ross-shire Electric Supply Co Ltd. The company were now able to supply power to much of Mid-Ross and Easter Ross. The following year, the firm extended cables to Tain, serving a total population of 15,000.

Ross County Football Club was officially constituted on 31st July 1929. Two weeks later the club opened their new ground and stand at Dingwall, and to cap it all, beat Inverness Caley in their first-ever Highland League game!

Kyle Golf Course was opened. The course was laid out on land at the Plock, donated by Sir Daniel Hamilton.

Another Church Union

The United Free Church merged with the Church of Scotland and as a result a number of churches, mostly built by United Free congregations in the last thirty years, became disused. Several older buildings, however, such as the 'parliamentary' church at Ullapool, also became redundant.

The Local Government (Scotland) Act abolished parish councils, transferring their duties to County Councils from 1930.

> **Go West, Young Man**
>
> Regular press advertisements in the late 1920s encouraged 'boy settlers', including school-leavers of 14, to emigrate to Canada to take farm work. Free or reduced passages and accommodation in 'approved farm homes' were offered.

Old Days in Ullapool

West Argyle Street

Looking up Quay Street from the harbour, with the old Tanera Cafe on the left

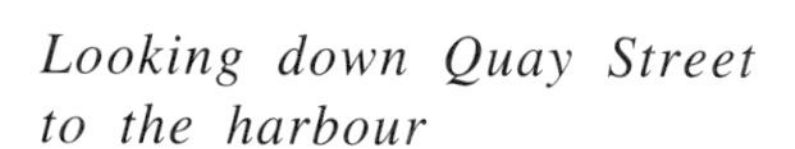

Looking down Quay Street to the harbour

Childhood in the 1920s

BARBARA MACLENNAN grew up in Coigach, one of thirteen children of whom the first seven were boys.

"My father eventually became very anxious for a girl," she recalled, "to keep my mother company and help about the house."

Her grandfather was *Coinneach a'phuist*, 'Kenneth the post', in the late 19th century. "He carried the mail for Coigach a dozen miles daily from Ullapool, along the steep path which crosses the Big Rock. In turn, my uncle Murdo became the postman."

Barbara's first home was a black house at Reiff, but when she was two, in 1920, the family moved a few miles east to Laide.

"The new house was marvellous, with a slate roof instead of thatch. We moved by horse and cart, along with our three cows and other animals."

The house had been bought for the family for £100, by two uncles who had left the district and done well. Barbara's father retained his old croft at Reiff, and was able to add stock on his new land.

Life at Home

The house soon became a home from home. Barbara's mother kept it spotless, and there were always colourful plants.

"She baked scones every day and once a week, if there was sugar and eggs to spare, pancakes. She made cheese too. Rennet added to skimmed milk produced creamed cheese, which was strained for several days, then placed in round containers under pressure for several more days. As many as a dozen cheeses could be drying out on the staircase at one time."

Her mother also made the clothes which the family wore. Wool from their sheep was sent annually to JM.Hunter of Brora. In spring, blankets were taken to a nearby burn to be washed, stamped in a tub then rinsed and left to dry on dykes or the grass.

"From June to September we walked barefoot. Come the autumn we all, boys and girls, wore tackety boots, and took great pride in them!"

Crofting, Fishing and Food

Once a year the family's cows were sent to nearby Achnahaird, to be served by a bull provided by the Board of Agriculture.

When it came time for the lambs to be sent to market, Barbara's father would shepherd them all the way to Dingwall, eighty miles away. A sheep was killed once a year for food.

"Sheep's head broth was made afterwards. It was delicious and very good for you. Every second year a bull calf was also raised for killing. Beef would be salted and hung to cure, and eaten over the winter.

In 1995, approaching her 80th birthday, Barbara MacLennan recalled happy days of childhood in a very different world in the 1920s.

"Every corner of the local croft lands was cultivated. We grew turnips, carrots, corn and hay. The turnips were chopped up, put in buckets and given to the cows.

"There would be three great stooks of corn outdoors, while a massive amount of hay was stored in the barn. Corncrakes, now quite rare, used to come down and gobble up the stray bits from the stooks."

From Monday to Saturday the family usually ate fish, mainly cod and herring. Barbara's father was a keen fisherman, having sailed on east-coast herring boats. He continued to fish until he was 70.

"He was a skipper during the salmon fishing season, sailing from Reiff on a flat-bottomed boat. The salmon fishermen used to take the catch to the local bothy, then to the ice house at Badentarbet to be wrapped in *shelister* and shipped to Billingsgate market. They were huge fish, and fishing brought in a useful wage."

A barrel of herring arrived from the east coast at the start of winter. Barbara herself used to catch cuddies (young saith) in the evenings. "You could stand on rocks and just literally pick them up. Now you won't see any fish at all in the sea close to shore. The boys also used to fish for lobsters, and made their own creels."

On Sundays beef was eaten, mostly boiled rather than roasted, as ovens were not so efficient. Occasionally pork was also eaten, as a few neighbours kept pigs.

Supplies were also bought from the Dornie shopkeeper. "He had a horse-drawn van, and when he called we would buy a sack of oatmeal or flour, which we stored in wooden barrels with lids. If we had no money he would give us credit."

Water was carried in pails from a nearby spring, covered over as a well.

Religion and Discipline

Religion was keenly observed in the home. The children were taught their catechism and Commandments before they went to school.

"Father would read us a chapter of the Bible every day, and the whole family would sing a Psalm. We lived according to Christian principles, but there was still a lot of humour."

House calls by the minister were awesome occasions. "He cut such a solemn figure, with his great black hat and umbrella. I remember once saying to my sister, who was playing with his umbrella, *'Se sin umbrella, a' cruitheader'* - 'You mustn't do that, that's God's umbrella!'

"Discipline was strict. My mother never smacked, but father certainly did if roused. His technique was to give a quick flick with a switch - after that we were well behaved!"

Though life was quite hard, the family were usually healthy, but there was a terrible time when Barbara's sister died from scarlet fever and her brother contracted the much-feared illness.

"My brother was so ill that father rowed to Lochinver to summon Dr Turner, who was revered locally. After his visit, the doctor left his clothes on the beach as the disease was so infectious. Happily my brother recovered, but I still think it was not so much medicine he was given by the doctor as courage."

Schooldays

Barbara attended Altandubh School until the age of 12, when she won a bursary to attend Ullapool Higher Grade School.

"It was worth £13 a term, and such awards had not long started up then, so I was lucky. I certainly would not say I was the bright one of the family either."

Barbara spent each term in Ullapool without seeing her family. Her brother Kenneth, a forestry worker at Braemore, would then take her home on his motorbike. She left school at 15 - enabling her sister to follow her to Ullapool, as bursaries were not available to members of one family at the same time - and went to work in Glasgow before, aged 18, she could at last enter her chosen profession of nursing. Meantime her father died, and Kenneth quit forestry to run the croft.

"Unfortunately, my father had not left a will assigning the croft to him, so he could not be registered. Kenneth became a second father to us, so it was a terrible shock when he died in 1937."

After qualifying, Barbara was posted to Italy to deal with troops injured in the front line. Returning to Ross-shire, she worked at the Ross Memorial Hospital, Dingwall, before pursuing a career with SSAFA, for which she received the MBE. Barbara MacLennan eventually retired to live in Ullapool. She died in 2001.

George Washington Wilson

Above: Charlestown, Gairloch, looking towards Flowerdale, at the turn of the century
Below: Poolewe, also around the turn of the century

George Washington Wilson

Diary of a Year

1930

Call for Piers

An appeal for a new pier at Applecross was made by one of the local ministers, who complained about the existing arrangement where a rowing-boat met MacBrayne's Stornoway-Kyle steamer at sea during the small hours of the morning. The MacBrayne boat was unable to use the pier due to tidal limitations.

At this time, Applecross people had two other ways in and out of the area, by land over the frequently impassable Bealach na Ba track, or by another boat the *Passing Cloud*, owned by the Wills family, the new owners of Applecross Estate, which made a twice-weekly 'shopping' trip to Kyle.

Calls were also made in 1930 for piers at Little Loch Broom and Glenelg.

Death of a War Veteran

Hugh Mackenzie of Lochcarron, popularly known as 'Hughack', died at the age of 34. He had been badly injured in the war while serving with the Ross Mountain Battery and never fully recovered, but carried on his daily life uncomplainingly, running a general stores in the village. Before burial, his coffin was met at Tullich by a large number of the community, and carried in sombre procession from there to the churchyard.

Distress Fund

It was reported in February that, following the widespread failure of the previous year's crops, hardship was being experienced in the West Highlands. The Departments of Health and Agriculture made representations to trustees of the Highlands & Islands Distress Fund (dating from the 19th century) for help.

A mass meeting of Ross-shire crofters, farmworkers, farmers and landowners was held in Dingwall in January to discuss a crisis of low prices and wages. The meeting inspired a national campaign involving thousands of farmworkers.

Television Demonstration

Wireless enthusiasts and all those interested in its wonders should muster in force tonight when Mr Dinsdale will lecture on "television" and demonstrate this latest wonderful development of the power of the ether.

Ross-shire Journal, February

Dornie Developments

A new water scheme was inaugurated at Dornie in May, at a ceremony attended by a large gathering. In the same month, a provisional order was obtained by the South-West Ross District Committee of the County Council for a bridge over Loch Long. It would take ten years and much campaigning to have it finally built.

The remote Altnaharrie Inn on the west shore of Loch Broom became a private house for the Mitford family. The ferry to Ullapool continued to operate; and the inn re-opened in the 1970s, achieving international fame for its food.

Dramatic Effects

During a severe storm, the *Ross-shire Journal* reported that overhead tension wires in Strathpeffer 'flashed vividly'.

Football Specials

There was great excitement in March as Ross-shire's new senior football team, Ross County, played Elgin in the North of Scotland Cup Final. To meet demand from west coast supporters, a service of "football special trains" was run from Kyle to Inverness, where the final was to be played. To cap the day, Ross County won the match 2-0 and the team returned to an enthusiastic reception in Dingwall.

Vehicles Great and Small

A table of tariffs published by Ross & Cromarty County Council for ferry services at Strome, Dornie and Totaig illustrated the wide variety of transport in 1930. Fares were listed for motor-car, charabanc, motor-cycle, motor-cycle-with-sidecar, bicycle, horse-and-cart, horse-and-four-wheeler, carriage-and-pair, furniture (per boat-load), horses, cattle and sheep, as well as foot-passengers.

Timber Operations

An Inverness timber merchant completed a two-year contract felling trees in Dundonnell Woods and demolished several temporary sawmills. Messrs James Jones & Sons of Larbert were reported to be felling around Gairloch in August. In the autumn, a puffer made a number of visits to Lochcarron to load logs.

Cod in Short Supply

In March the cod-fishing season at Gairloch was reported to have been disappointing to date.

Facility Opens

A storage tank with a capacity of 250,000 gallons was built at Kyle to supply ships with oil.

New Councils Set Up

Four district councils were set up in Wester Ross in succession to the former district committees and parish councils. Thus Lochbroom, Gairloch, Lochcarron and South West Ross District Councils took office. The role of parish councils in levying local rates was taken over by the County Council. Responsibility for roads was assumed by the Highways Committee of the County Council.

Call for Local Schools

The work of the Ross-shire Education Authority was taken over by the County Council Education Committee. Before being wound up, the Education Authority suggested it would be best if west-coast secondary pupils could receive their education at local schools rather than at Dingwall. In this thinking they were some fifty years ahead of their time.

Shinty's Poor Prospects?

The *Ross-shire Journal* was concerned for the future of shinty in Lochcarron.

Though for years a stronghold of shinty, Lochcarron is apparently passing through a transition stage. Will the boys who with their camans carry on daily feuds, regain the former greatness of the parish in their national game? Or will they join the throng and take up the popular game of football?

Perish the thought! But the writer need not have worried - in the 1930s Lochcarron won several trophies and, despite low periods, the club survived to enjoy its best season in 1999-2000.

1930 (continued)

Talc Mine Opens

In an unusual industrial venture, a mine producing talc was opened in 1930 at Ardintoul on the south shore of Loch Alsh, opposite Auchtertyre. The market for talc was a valuable one, worth £125 per ton at the time.

Owned by Northern Mining Company, the mine was reported in full production that summer. Situated on a hillside about 100 feet above sea level, it was connected to the shore by an aerial ropeway. More than 100 tons of talc had been brought down by June, and made ready for shipment.

The *Ross-shire Journal* reported:

The first full cargo will be conveyed south next week. Great interest has been taken in the discovery of the talc, and many prospectors have been searching neighbouring mountains. So far, no other mineral has been found in quantities sufficient to warrant operations.

The mine ceased operating about 1950 on the death of the company's owner, and following the loss of a boat carrying a full cargo off Sleat.

School Re-opens

Craig School was re-opened after the school roll rose to five, following the arrival in the district of a forestry worker and his family.

The re-appearance of scarlet fever in Lochcarron caused great anxiety.

Cooking by Electricity

Ross-shire Electric Supply Co Ltd gave a demonstration of the advantages of cooking by electricity at their show-rooms in Church Street, Dingwall.

Sunday Trains Run

A service of excursion trains was operated on the Kyle line on Sundays for the first time ever during 1930. It proved a popular innovation, with the first train attracting 350 passengers, many of whom took the chance to cross to Skye. An adult return fare from Inverness was 3s 6d.

There was considerable opposition, however. In conjunction with the new Sunday service, the proprietor of the Station Hotel at Achnasheen started a motor excursion bus service taking passengers to Loch Maree or Gairloch, for 5s. or 7s.6d. return. This prompted ill feeling in Gairloch, where a joint meeting of the three local church congregations was held at the Drill Hall. The train service continued to operate, however, until October.

There were also fears of trouble on Skye, where the first trippers were escorted by a police constable from Broadford. But the *Ross-shire Journal* reported there was no reaction "apart from a sullen look here and there".

Showing a willingness to respond to local demand, the LMS also ran a special late-evening train to take local senior and junior choirs and their parents from Strathcarron to Kyle to attend the South-West Ross Mod.

"Come to Scotland" Campaign

As part of a national 'Come to Scotland' campaign aimed at attracting more tourists, the LMS provided an extra train service between Inverness and Kyle, connecting with an additional service between Glasgow, Edinburgh and the Highlands. The Kyle train included a refreshment car. Connections were provided by bus from Garve to Ullapool and Achnasheen to Gairloch, and by boat from Kyle to Skye.

The likely viability of an air service between Kyle and Lewis was discussed.

Kenneth Cameron, Ullapool, retired from the County Council after many years and received tributes for bringing new transport facilities to Lochbroom since the turn of the century: piers at Badentarbet, Scoraig and Ullapool; new roads to Reiff, Culnacraig, Badluarach and Badralloch; and new paths to Scoraig and Achmore.

Reasons to be Cheerless

The *Ross-shire Journal* saw little cause for cheer at the start of 1930. Noting the continuing fall in population, it commented:

"With few exceptions, village life is a shadow of what it was two or three decades ago. Is there no remedy at all?

"Afforestation? Yes, but half a century will have gone before a hundred families stand provided by such development at the rate of progress ordinarily possible.

"Tourists? Yes, but except for a fleeting visit and an occasional purchase, wherein will extended tourist traffic definitely help settle a larger, well employed resident population?

"The fishing industry also is passing through a parlous period. Population is falling off in fishing villages everywhere. Young fishermen are not following in the footsteps of their fathers."

Only the introduction of industries could help to bring steady work and wages and "settle a fixed population in the far north." The paper set great store by hydro-electric projects, deploring the opposition of certain interests which had prevented several schemes from being developed.

Nursing and Health Care

In August 1930 Lochalsh Nursing Association reported that, since the District Nurse Miss MacFadyen had been provided with a motor-car in 1929, she had been able to make 410 more visits than in the previous year (eight extra visits per week), while reducing her working hours by 860 (or 16 hours a week).

Local nursing associations had been established for some years in Wester Ross. They were charitable bodies, each supporting and financing the work of several nurses. The Federation of Ross & Cromarty Parish & District Nursing Associations had recently been formed, its committee including stalwarts of voluntary work such as Mrs Murray of Lochcarron Estate, Lady Marjory Mackenzie of Gairloch Estate, and Mrs Fraser of Leckmelm Estate.

Lochbroom Nursing Association was the oldest in the north-west Highlands, and currently supported three nurses.

In these days before the National Health Service, patients were still liable to pay for medical attention. Working men were expected to contribute to insurance schemes administered by public bodies such as the Health Insurance & Medical Service Board and the Scottish Department of Public Health.

Insurance covered only men, and visits by doctors to their families were chargeable. However, in practice doctors often waived payment. Nor was there a charge if a nurse attended first before calling out the doctor.

Successful Shows

The annual Highland Village Industries Exhibition was held in Kyle and, as usual, reported a great success.

North Gairloch Annual Crofters' Show was held in September at Laide. Competition categories included scones, oatcakes, eggs, butter, cheese, crowdie, jam, potatoes, turnips, cabbages, flowers, wool, stockings, socks and fleeces, in addition to the usual livestock categories such as cattle, sheep, ponies and poultry.

Fish Market Opens

Negotiations between Ullapool Pier Trustees and a Glasgow fisherman led to the setting-up of a white-fish market at the harbour. It was noted that there was currently only limited local demand for white fish, and it was hoped the market would attract buyers from elsewhere.

Joy to Humble Homes

While in Burma during 1930, Lady Gibb, owner of Gruinard Estate, sent boxes of tea for distribution among the elderly and needy in townships around Little Loch Broom. The *Ross-shire Journal* paid tribute.

Not only does Lady Gibb remember residents in the district at Christmas but also during the season, when Her Ladyship makes a point of visiting many of the old and sick, and also distributes large quantities of venison and rabbits. Lady Gibb's presence in many humble homes brings joy and comfort.

Before being wound up in 1930, Gairloch Parish Council paid tribute to their late chairman Sir Kenneth Mackenzie of Gairloch Estate. His son Sir Hector became chairman briefly.

A puffer unloaded 120 tons of coal for local merchant Colin Gunn at Gairloch pier on 22nd September.

Unmusical Interlude

During the weekend, the SS Claymore lay at Gairloch pier. As usual she carried a large complement of tourists. On Sunday night, a selection of the trippers shattered the peace by giving lusty, ribald and unmusical renderings of well-known Scotch songs of rather questionable origin. Naturally all the residents within range were rather shocked.

Ross-shire Journal, 26th September

The death was reported of Roderick Mackenzie, former teacher at Bordbuie School, Dundonnell, and latterly gardener at Braemore, whose stories of local history and customs were saved and published as *Tales and Legends of Lochbroom.*

Bus Services

The daily seasonal bus service between Gairloch and Achnasheen, operated by Messrs Mackenzie Bros of Port Henderson, finished running for the year in late October.

A new motor-bus service started operating between Coigach and Dingwall on Wednesdays only, leaving Achiltibuie at 7.30am and returning from Dingwall at 6pm.

Poaching Cases

Several Torridon men appeared in court and were fined between 10s and £1 for killing stags. Six Ullapool men were fined between £1 and £5 for poaching salmon by boat and net in the estuary of the Ullapool river, after charges were brought by Mr Rose of Rhidorroch Estate.

Horses were still vital in day-to-day life in Wester Ross at this time, to work the land and for transport. At the monthly horse sales in Dingwall, Clydesdales fetched between 20 and 25 guineas, while 'work horses' sold for around five guineas. Carriages, harnesses and other accessories were also sold.

Appeal for a Road

Residents of Loggie, Lochbroom, complained to the County Council about the lack of a road to the township. The only access was a footpath from the present road-end at Letters. The Highways Committee passed the request to Lochbroom District Council, encouraging them to seek grants to build the road themselves. The County Council would then be prepared to maintain it.

Upstairs Downstairs

Domestic service was still an important source of employment in 1930. Mr and Mrs Kemble, owners of Duncraig Castle, employed eight indoor staff, comprising a cook and kitchenmaid, two housemaids, an under-housemaid, parlour-maid, laundrymaid and sewing maid. They also employed a head gardener and under-gardener.

St Kilda Evacuated

The inhabitants of Wester Ross were used to seeing young people leave to improve their prospects. However, some workers did move into the area as well, to take up jobs in forestry. One such was Neil Ferguson, who moved to Stromeferry in September to work for the Forestry Commission, accompanied by his wife and father-in-law.

Their background was unusual, for they were among the last of the native population to leave St Kilda.

The plight of the St Kildans had given cause for concern throughout 1930. In February, the beleaguered community was relieved after four months cut off from the outside world when a Fishery Board cruiser finally got through with food, mail and medical supplies. Dr Shearer of the Board of Health later reported that, of 38 inhabitants on the island, only 15 (including children) were males. He feared it would not be long before there were not enough men left to sail the boats.

The *Ross-shire Journal* agreed at the time that the islanders' future was bleak.

Obviously the time has come when steps should be taken to encourage the remaining islanders to seek a home elsewhere. Such transference must be voluntary. Can the wisdom of the step be in doubt? The spirit of patriotism makes the islanders cling to their inhospitable rock, and their sentiment is not blameworthy, although the wisdom of it may well be challenged.

In July, the St Kildans agreed to leave the island. The Board of Agriculture began arranging for land to be made available, with 28 people expected to move to Mull, and eight to Skye. One person wished to move to Glasgow and another to Inverness.

The heartbreaking evacuation was complete in September. In the event Wester Ross welcomed perhaps its most unusual settlers. St Kilda remained deserted from 1931 until 1957, when a tracking station was set up in connection with the South Uist rocket range, occasionally manned by Ministry of Defence staff.

New Links to the Outside World

An item from the *Ross-shire Journal* in March 1930 illustrates how adaptable people were in those days, and how far communications technology has advanced since.

Kyle subscribers have been unable to phone the doctor after 8pm owing to the fact that his telephone is connected with the Balmacara exchange, which closes at 8pm. But thanks to the energy of Mr Kindness, the Postmaster, arrangements have now been made to connect the doctor's telephone with one in the Kyle Hotel during the night hours. Mrs Mackenzie, Kyle Hotel, has kindly given full use of her telephone for the purpose, and anyone requiring the doctor's services after 8pm should communicate with her.

It was a great day for every community when it was at last connected by telephone to the outside world.

Major improvements were made during the course of 1930. In April, Ian Macpherson, MP for Ross-shire, was advised by the Postmaster-General that he had authorised new telephone cables to be laid between Dingwall and Skye via Lochcarron and Kyle; between Dingwall and Poolewe via Achnasheen, Kinlochewe and Gairloch; and between Dingwall and Ullapool. That autumn, all these places in turn were connected to the trunk system. Exchanges in each district were financed by local subscribers.

In August Kyle obtained its link with the outside world, followed in September by Lochcarron, where fifteen subscribers gathered in the new exchange to hear the Kyle Postmaster make the first trunk telephone call to Inverness.

At a meeting of subscribers in Ullapool a few days later Mr Leitch, the Dingwall Postmaster, presided while the first trunk call was made to the Provost of Dingwall. Kenneth Cameron, former chairman of the old Lochbroom Parish Council, welcomed a development which, he said, local people had been requesting for twenty years.

In October, subscribers at Gairloch met to hear Dr Knox put through the first trunk call to Member of Parliament Mr Macpherson at his home in faraway London.

Eilean Donan Castle: Symbol of the Highlands

It is probably the most photographed building in the Highlands: a ruggedly inspiring symbol of centuries-old clan battles and Jacobite uprisings. And yet it is only a magnificent replica, dating from 1932.

Until the First World War, the previous incarnation of Eilean Donan Castle had been a gaunt ruin for nearly two centuries, since three government warships shelled it and their crews plundered it during the Jacobite rising of 1719.

Eilean Donan Castle was always associated with the MacRaes, the men-at-arms of the Mackenzies of Kintail, whose stronghold it was. In 1509 the MacRaes were officially appointed Constables of the Castle. In 1539 they defended it against an attack by the powerful Macdonalds, led by Donald Gorm, who was killed.

Vision

By the end of the 19th century, a vision had formed in the mind of one local man, John MacRae of Conchra, to restore the forlorn ruin to its former glory.

The MacRaes of Conchra were one of two branches of the MacRae clan, the other being the MacRaes of Inverinate. John was a second son; his elder brother fought a famous case in the early 1900s to be recognised as overall chieftain of the clan, but the Lord Lyon King of Arms preferred the Inverinate MacRaes' claim.

How History was Re-created

Be that as it may, all MacRaes were no doubt interested to learn of John's plans for the old castle. Born in 1861, he had married Isabella Gilstrap in 1889 and agreed to take her name after his own as a requirement for her to inherit a family fortune. When Isabella's uncle died she became a wealthy woman. By then, she shared her husband's enthusiasm for restoring the castle - and she had the money to finance the project.

It was not until 1913 that they were able to purchase the little island and its ruin from Sir Keith Fraser of Inverinate. On 14th August 1913, Major MacRae-Gilstrap, as he now was, held a symbolic gathering of MacRaes amid the ruins.

His next steps were the most important. He appointed George Mackie Watson as architect, and Farquhar MacRae from Avernish as a mason in charge of the re-building work.

Farquhar MacRae had already had a remarkable dream in which he visualised the former castle in detail. From this he had drawn up a plan.

Watson's final design was based on an actual plan which, as luck would have it, was found in Edinburgh at this time. It was uncannily similar to MacRae's vision.

Fruition

It took nearly twenty years for Farquhar MacRae and his men to complete the restoration. Sadly, he himself died shortly before the building was formally opened in July 1932.

The castle's two principal rooms are the billeting room and banqueting hall. An interesting exhibit is the original iron gate dating from the 13th century, which was discovered in the castle's well during the reconstruction.

A 'modern' feature is the three-arched bridge leading to the building, which did not feature in the original plan. It was added after the main restoration work was completed.

John MacRae-Gilstrap died in 1937, when his son Duncan inherited the castle. Duncan was not required to use the Gilstrap name, so the family were once again plain MacRaes.

Duncan's son John decided to open the castle to the public in 1955, when the family moved out. John MacRae set up the Conchra Charitable Trust to look after the building in 1983. One maintenance problem which faces the Trust from time to time is erosion, arising from the use of local sea-sand in the reconstruction.

Eilean Donan Castle is open to the public from April to November. The castle is also now a popular venue for private family gatherings and weddings.

Above: The yacht Passing Cloud *(see under 1930) belonged to the Wills family, owners of Applecross Estate. Mr Beaton was the skipper, with other estate staff as crew in rotation. In summer she was re-rigged and took house guests round the islands*

Below: Eilean Donan Castle

The Thirties

The few inhabitants remaining on Tanera Mor decided life on the island was no longer viable and abandoned their homes to settle on the mainland. The population had been over seventy strong in 1901.

The telephone network was extended from Ullapool to Dundonnell Post Office. From there it was planned to provide links to townships round Little Loch Broom.

With the restoration of Eilean Donan Castle completed after 20 years, it was formally opened on 22nd July. The Macrae-Gilstrap family made it their home until 1955 *(see p.36)*.

Residents of Cuaig, Calnacille and Lonbain in North Applecross petitioned Ross & Cromarty County Council in July for help. Since the end of the war, supplies had been brought into the district by a fortnightly steamer service from Kyle, provided by the Department of Agriculture. Recently, however, there had been a change: goods were now brought to Strathcarron Station by train, then by road to Shieldaig and thence by boat but only as far as Fearnmore. In bad weather, the coastal townships further south were having difficulty getting to Fearnmore to pick up their supplies. Residents appealed for either a new road around the coast or a motor-boat service from Kyle. In August a deputation attended a meeting in Kyle to discuss the problems, but they had little joy; many years later the Applecross minister noted that the same arrangements were still in place.

On her death in April, Lady Seaforth left £800,000 to charities, incuding £60,000 to the Seaforth Sanatorium, which had opened at Brahan in 1908.

A new village hall was opened at Balmacara, a gift from the laird Sir Daniel Hamilton.

Plockton Small Boat Sailing Club was formed. The club holds a very popular regatta fortnight in August, a highlight of the west coast sailing calendar.

Lael Forest Garden was created by the Forestry Commission near Braemore.

Dr Charles Ferguson was appointed district medical officer at Lochcarron. He was to be the local GP for the next 42 years.

The death of the renowned Gaelic poet Alexander Cameron, known as the Tournaig Bard, was announced. A monument to him was later erected at Inverewe.

A Junior Gaelic Mod was staged at Leckmelm in July.

Mrs Mackenzie of the Caledonian Hotel, Ullapool, entertained friends and staff to a musical evening to mark the end of a successful tourist season.

Shipping News

The steamers Loch Broom and Loch Dunvegan called at Ullapool pier during the week, the former with a consignment of tar and the latter with the usual general cargo from Glasgow. The lighter Inchcolm discharged a full cargo of coals at Ullapool and at the south side of the loch.

Ross-shire Journal, October 1933

1934

Plockton Village Hall was opened at a ceremony attended by a large number of guests, who were entertained by the local Gaelic choir among others.

Social Life and Entertainment, 1931

IN AN AGE long before the joys of television and radio reached Wester Ross, local people found many ways to entertain themselves.

The following events were just some of those held in the darkest and bleakest months of the year between mid-January and mid-March 1931. This was, it might be added, a particularly snowy winter, and people did not have cars to get around, so going out involved a special effort.

In January and February, Lochcarron Shinty Club held dances, with music performed by local musicians.

Kyle Territorials (B Company, 4/5th Seaforths) held their annual dance at the Drill Hall. Lochbroom branch of An Comunn Gaidhealach held a concert and dance. Lochcarron W.R.I. arranged a demonstration of quilting and knitting, with a cake competition. Tea was served afterwards, and the National Anthem sung, as was the custom at many social occasions. Also in Lochcarron, a whist drive was held, followed by a tea then a dance.

Ullapool W.R.I. organised an entertainment of sketches and songs at the Drill Hall, followed by a dance. Their next meeting featured a demonstration of scone-making and a lecture on the care of young children, followed by a tea and then dancing to eightsome reels.

Gairloch branch of An Comunn Gaidhealach held monthly ceilidhs, and in February hosted a talk with a musical interlude.

A concert was held in Poolewe Drill Hall in aid of the Gairloch Nursing Association, with piping, singing, dancing and sketches put on by Inverasdale School pupils. At the end, Dr Knox thanked the audience for the money raised, which was to help purchase a car for the nurse.

A whist drive and dance was held at Gairloch Drill Hall in support of the National Mod, due to take place at Dingwall. A concert at Lochcarron Drill Hall was also held in aid of the Mod, with a dance and tea afterwards.

Music at most events was performed by local musicians, playing traditional instruments, mainly fiddle or bagpipes.

Shinty was played when the weather permitted, for example Lochcarron against a team from Achnasheen. Football was ever-popular: games in these weeks included Strath against a combined team from Sand, Erradale and Melvaig, and Ullapool against Braemore.

Football spectating was also popular now that Ross County was a senior club. In January, a special train took 150 supporters to watch the team play in Inverness, with 70 fans boarding at Kyle, 30 at Plockton and 40 at Strathcarron.

1935

Frank Fraser Darling carried out a study of red deer at Dundonnell from 1935 to 1937. He later directed the Red Deer Survey during the 1950s, a comprehensive study of one of the Highlands' native species.

A new Order authorised construction of a bridge across Loch Long at Dornie, but once again hopes were to be frustrated until 1940, when Kyle's importance as a war-time naval base helped clinch the case for a bridge to replace the ferry.

The former school building on Market Street, Ullapool, now the village hall, was re-furbished. In summer-time, the hall was made available as accommodation for youth hostellers, an arrangement which continued for some years.

The Herring Industry Board was established. One of its remits was to promote specific landing ports, which in turn would dictate where fish-buyers were based.

The Caledonian Power Scheme, which proposed the production of calcium carbide through hydro-electricity - a project with a potentially significant effect for employment in the Highlands - was blocked by local authorities. For years afterwards the Highland press regretted the opportunity which had been lost.

Weaving a Success Story

In June 1937 it was reported that the Strome Weaving Factory, nowadays internationally known as Lochcarron Weavers, had been revived through the efforts of Mr C.W.Murray, owner of Lochcarron Estate.

He had approached Highland Home Industries Ltd, who had in turn put him in touch with Mr J.Morris Buchan, who owned a handloom mill in the Borders town of Galashiels. Mr Buchan agreed to rent the factory in Strome and sent a weaver, Mr Wood. He also promised that suitable local boys would be eligible for training at the Technical College in Galashiels.

Tweeds and blankets made at North Strome were first exhibited at the Highland Home Industries Exhibition, Kyle in 1939.

From 1949 the Strome factory produced tartans using Hattersley looms and yarn sent by the parent company in Galashiels. These proved a great success. The parent company subsequently adopted the trading name *Lochcarron of Scotland*, keeping its base in the Borders but opening premises around the Highlands and even overseas. By the end of the century the Strome factory and shop were still going strong. The chairman of *Lochcarron of Scotland* in 2000 was a Mr Buchan - son of the original mill-owner.

1936

The present-day Inverewe House was built for Mrs Sawyer.

The Highland Development League was set up as a movement to promote ways of encouraging agriculture, fishing and other economic activities in the Highlands during these difficult years. At the same time, the Scottish Economic Committee set up a sub-committee with similar aims. Money was set aside to promote Highland development - unfortunately the war intervened before it could be used.

1937

The old pier at Stromeferry, long derelict since its heyday at the end of the 19th century, was condemned as unsafe by the Board of Trade and demolished by its owners the LMS Railway.

1938

Already the threat of another war was felt in Ross-shire. In January 1938, Dingwall Town Council discussed possible precautions against air raids.

In a tragic accident off Applecross, three fishermen were drowned.

In October, Duncraig Castle was offered by Sir Daniel and Lady Hamilton to Ross and Cromarty County Council as a technical education college. Following the outbreak of war in 1939, however, the building was requisitioned and plans for the college put on hold.

1939

Britain declared war on Germany on 3rd September 1939. Local territorials were mobilised. The 4th Seaforths, as part of 152 (Highland) Brigade of the 51st Highland Division, were sent to Saarland to guard the Maginot Line *(see June 1940)*.

Work parties were set up in villages such as Lochcarron and Garve to organise home comforts for men away on service.

A small naval contingent arrived at Aultbea to begin establishing a naval base. Loch Ewe was to play a vital war-time role, particularly after the safety of Scapa Flow as a naval base was put in doubt by the sinking of HMS *Royal Oak* there in October.

However, it seemed no anchorage was safe. HMS *Nelson* was severely damaged by mines in Loch Ewe on 4th December.

A Trading Empire

In 1937 Commander Clair Vyner, a wealthy landowner based at Keanchulish near Ullapool, established a flour mill on Isle Martin. Two millers and their families were settled on the island, while workers came daily by boat from Ardmair.

At the same time Vyner established Lochbroom Trading Company Ltd, which during the next few years developed into a chain of bakeries and grocery shops throughout Wester Ross and elsewhere in the Highlands. The bakeries were supplied with flour from the Isle Martin mill. Vyner bought a vessel, *Penola*, which sailed between Glasgow and Isle Martin, taking wheat north and flour south.

At its height, the Lochbroom Trading Co Ltd numbered over twenty retail outlets. Seven were in Wester Ross: at Dornie, Kyle, Plockton, Lochcarron, Gairloch, Aultbea and Ullapool. There were others at Lochinver, Dingwall, Tain, Fearn, Bonar Bridge, Lairg, Embo, Wick, Thurso, Inverness, Lochboisdale, Tobermory, and Strontian.

During the war and in the years just after, the business lost money and Vyner broke it up. The flour mill was demolished. Commander Vyner continued to live at Keanchulish, just across from Isle Martin, and was a well respected figure until his death in 1989.

C.Allen

Above: The old side school and burial ground at Bordbuie, Dundonnell. The school closed in World War Two.

Below: The Bealach na Ba in early days of motoring

War was declared on 3rd September 1939. During 1940, rationing and other restrictions began to affect daily life at home. After March, Wester Ross was part of a "Protected Area" and proof of residence had to be shown when travelling.

Naval bases were established at Kyle and Aultbea. Kyle became the main British mine-laying base (HMS Trelawney), with berths at the harbour restricted to naval vessels, which made life difficult for local fishermen. Crisis followed crisis during the year: the fall of Denmark, Norway, Belgium, Holland and France, the evacuation of Dunkirk, the Battle of Britain.

By the end of 1940 all men aged 18-36 had been called up. This was a dark time, when local and national concerns merged. It was also a time when people showed great resilience and determination.

Darkest Hour

1940

Bleak January

As everywhere else, the black-out was strictly enforced at night. At the start of the year, air attacks over Britain were as yet only sporadic. On New Year's Day two German planes attacked a British ship in the Shetlands; one was reported to have been shot down.

The press were forbidden to publish weather reports, even about conditions over previous days unless a full week had elapsed. It later emerged that January 1940 was the coldest since 1881.

Rationing Introduced

From January, sugar, bacon and butter were rationed. Meat was not rationed until March, but housewives were still required to register with a nominated butcher in January. Murdo MacGregor, a Dingwall butcher, advised customers: *You have got to register for butcher meat by 8th January. No comments, but you will get a square deal.*

The *Ross-shire Journal* reported that the county had survived the first week of rationing without problems. Supplies had been plentiful. *Surpluses rather than scarcity appear to have been the rule. Housewives may find the coupon system irksome or even irritating, but familiarity will help ease matters.*

Christmas for the Troops

Ullapool Charities Entertainment and Linen League sent Christmas boxes to 94 servicemen in December 1939. Each box contained *one iced Christmas cake with regimental badge, a large box of mixed biscuits, a box of sweets, a pair of socks or helmet, a pocket testament, and 50 cigarettes.* Non-smokers received (instead of cigarettes) a box of cheese, a packet of dates, a half-pound of chocolate, and a packet of stamped letter-cards. The pocket testament was inscribed with an "encouraging message" from Mrs Fraser, Leckmelm.

From 15th January, the Ministry of Food took over the purchase of all animals for slaughter, paying a fixed price. A Meat Controller was appointed in Dingwall, based at the auction mart.

Making More of the Land

The Agricultural Executive Committee announced that grants amounting to £2 per acre would be given to crofters to plough up grassland on condition that it had been grass for at least seven years. The aim was to ensure as much land as possible was sown for crops.

With so many men liable for call-up, the Agricultural Executive Committee announced the immediate recruitment of a Women's Land Army. It was arranged that grieves and foremen - "key men" on the land - would not be called up. Tractors were provided for ploughing, and deer-forest land allocated for grazing.

In an effort to increase egg production, the Committee urged the culling of 'unproductive poultry'.

The Garve Work Society sent £5 to Finnish troops currently resisting Soviet invasion. A number of other fund-rasing events were staged for the Finns.

Two Kyle-bound trains were de-railed near Dingwall in January and February respectively, killing or injuring 50 sheep. The sheep had been sent to Stornoway by order of the Dingwall Meat Controller.

The farthing was brought back into circulation as a means of preventing overcharging.

The War Secretary announced that the kilt would no longer be worn by troops, and would be replaced by battledress. *For walking out, all ranks in possession of kilts will wear them until they are worn out. There will be no further issue of kilts during the war except to pipers and drummers.*

The County Council appointed an Air Raid Precautions Committee, and discussed the availability of gas masks.

A Ross-shire branch of the National Savings Committee was set up.

Severe storms caused damage in February. The wooden pier at the head of Loch Broom, built by German prisoners during the last war, was wrecked, floating down the loch in two pieces, which were caught by locals and used for firewood.

Canteen Ladies Return

Dingwall Canteen Ladies served tea to servicemen on all trains passing through the town's railway station. This practice would continue throughout the war, as it had during the 1914-18 conflict.

The Ministry of Supply urged the public to save waste-paper. Commenting on the high price of newsprint, the *Ross-shire Journal* regretted that it would no longer be possible to supply newsagents with the paper on a sale-or-return basis.

The Lovat Scouts at War

The Lovat Scouts garrisoned the Faroe Isles during 1940-42, before undergoing specialist training in mountain warfare in 1942-44. They went into action in Italy in 1944-45, conducting long-range operations behind enemy lines, greatly assisting the advance of the 8th Army.

Lochcarron Work Party sent parcels to local men serving abroad. Children of the village knitted cuffs from oddments of wool and sent them to the Women's Royal Voluntary Service for distribution, and knitted blankets to be donated to hospitals.

Handloom weavers in the Highlands complained about a lack of wool. The price and distribution of wool was fixed by the Wool Controller, and was claimed to be unfair. The Wool Control Advisory Committee urged women to use thinner wool when knitting.

Travel Restricted

Protected Area Established

From Monday 11th March a new Government Order, *the Defence of the Realm Act, Protected Area Order,* designated much of Scotland as a prohibited area, including Wester Ross.

Public concern over possible effects of this order on travel and tourism prompted the War Minister to respond:

There is no reason why the new Order should discourage visitors to the Highlands and Islands, either for holiday or business purposes, by persons of satisfactory credentials.

Military pickets were on duty in protected areas from that Monday. Soldiers examined permits at road and rail junctions, and travellers by rail and bus from Inverness had to produce their pass or, if living within the protected area, a certificate of residence or identity card. Transit visas for those journeying to Orkney or Shetland were issued by a military control office in Inverness Railway Station.

It was reported there was heavy demand for the new Certificate of Residence and Identity Cards throughout Ross-shire. In April Dingwall Town Council wrote to the Secretary of State for Scotland and the local MP Malcolm Macdonald complaining that long delays were being experienced by people trying to obtain a permit to enter the Protected Area. The usual time taken to obtain either a certificate of residence or green identity card with photo was ten days. The Council suggested that the police rather than the military should administer the issuing of passports. The likely effect on tourists coming north remained a cause for concern.

1940 (continued)

The *Grow More Food* campaign encouraged children to create gardens at their schools. By April 1940, the *Dig for Victory* slogan was in regular use, and the Secretary of State for Scotland appointed a committee to encourage greater food production.

It was reported in March that, out of forty men from Lochalsh currently serving in the forces, the majority were with the 4th Battalion of the Seaforth Highlanders. Three were in the Royal Air Force.

Plans to enable crofters to purchase seeds or manure in bulk were circulated by the Scottish Agricultural Organisation Society to crofters, townships and grazings committees.

On 13th March the war in Finland ended in defeat for the Finns, who were forced to concede land to Russia.

The *Ross-shire Journal* carried many 'jobs vacant' adverts for farmworkers.

There were heavy air raids over Scapa Flow and the rest of Orkney on 16th March, causing the first civilian casualties of the war. There was also a raid on the Forth Bridge.

The Government announced that whisky output would be cut by two-thirds during 1940.

New Bridge at Poolewe

A new road bridge was built across the River Ewe at Poolewe to cope with increased traffic to and from nearby military bases. Kenneth C.Mackenzie recalls in his book *The River Ewe* that until then, the largest vehicles to cross the old bridge were the open-topped touring coaches or charabancs operated by MacRae & Dick, which came that way in the summer.

Mr Mackenzie also recalls a Commando unit being based for training at Inveran House. The Commanding Officer was greatly disliked; he insisted on training with live ammunition - and was shot dead during an exercise near the river, since when his ghost has been seen by a number of anglers!

(*The River Ewe* was published in 2000.)

Men born in 1914, or between 10th March and 6th April 1920, were called up in April. Already those born in 1915-19 had been conscripted. The new enlistment affected 972 Highland men.

Denmark and Norway were invaded by Germany on 12th April.

One consequence was a further shortage of newsprint in Britain, as most wood-pulp was imported from Norway.

It was announced that over 250,000 acres of grass had been ploughed for crops in nearly 20,000 individual schemes.

Boy Scouts in Ullapool began a weekly collection of scrap paper. Girl Guides throughout Britain raised funds for lifeboats and air ambulances.

A well-publicised sighting of the Loch Ness monster on 7th April brought a little light relief.

Due to a shortage of men, the minimum age for tractor-drivers on public roads was reduced from 21 to 17.

Householders in Ross-shire were invited to consider taking in evacuees.

The Budget imposed price rises on items including tobacco, whisky and beer, railway fares, telephone, and postage: the cost of a postcard stamp being doubled from 1d to 2d. A maximum price was set for items including eggs and herring, the latter at £4 18s. per cran. The Government took measures to encourage savings, including setting up Savings Groups in factories and offices.

Dingwall Town Council sought sites for public air-raid shelters.

Rationing News

There were constant updates on changes in personal allowances. In March it was announced that there would be no coupons for sausages, eggs or venison after the 26th. Butter allowance was doubled to eight ounces per week, but halved again in May - then cut further to just 2oz. Meat allowance rose at that time to 2s.2d. a week. In September, due to a shortage of tea, people were asked to drink coffee instead. And so it went on - for 14 years.

Children without Fathers

Two Emergency Officers for Ross-shire - one for boys, one for girls - were apppointed in May, as in other counties, to improve juvenile welfare. There was concern over the growing numbers of young children whose fathers were away on active service. Volunteers were invited to spend time with such children.

The *Ross-shire Journal* called for a road to be built between Strathcarron and Stromeferry after the war. A survey had been carried out in the late 1930s.

Belgium and Holland were invaded by Germany on 10th May. Churchill became Prime Minister the next day.

Ross & Cromarty County Council and Inverness Town Council announced they would in future jointly operate the Kessock ferry. One councillor expressed the hope that they would make a better job of it than the Strome ferry, where he had sometimes found that "the men who should be attending to the boat were busy hay-making".

Despite the war, Strathpeffer Spa re-opened for the season on 6th May.

Because of increased munitions production, the number of unemployed fell by May 1940 from 1.5 million at the start of the war to less than a million.

Dornie Bridge Opens

The Dornie Bridge was formally opened on 30th April at a ceremony attended by 400 guests. The proceedings were presided over by Mr Charles Murray, Lochcarron, and a ribbon cut by Colin Campbell, Shiel House, who commented that an old prophecy was being fulfilled - *that the people of Kintail will one day walk dry-shod into Lochalsh.*

Later, at a lunch in the Loch Duich Hotel, Duncan MacPherson, the Kyle chemist and well-known publisher, toasted the bridge's success and thanked Murray, Campbell and the former South-West Ross District Committee for taking the fight for it as far as London and Edinbugh.

But after all, he added, *we have never been able to get anything in the west without a fight.*

The bridge was built at a cost of £60,000. For some years, drivers were required to pay a toll to cross it.

Gather Moss

The Ministry of Health and Red Cross Society appealed for sphagnum moss to be collected, for use in making dressings. A collection depot was established at Fortrose, and local work parties met each week at Kildary, Rosemarkie and Fortrose to prepare the dressings.

At a meeting of Lochbroom District Council, Mr Vyner of Lochbroom Trading Company offered to convey waste-paper and other scrap to appropriate markets in his boat *Penola* free of charge.

Farmworkers aged 21 or over were declared to be in a reserved occupation, and therefore no longer liable for call-up.

The Caledonian Park football pitch in Ullapool was ploughed up and planted. This was later the site of the Far Isles Bar.

Because of the labour shortage, schoolboys were invited to holiday work camps on farms and forest plantations.

Farmers who failed to plough a set acreage of land were now fined by the local Agricultural Executive Committee.

On the Front Line

Disaster at St Valery-en-Caux

On 4th June 1940, the same day that the evacuation of Dunkirk was completed, men of the 51st Highland Division, including the 4th Seaforth Highlanders, were fighting a desperate rearguard action against the Germans. The troops, who had been garrisoning the Maginot line earlier in the year, had been by-passed by the Germans as they occupied the Low Countries and France further north. Falling back, the 4th Seaforths and 4th Camerons counter-attacked the Germans at Abbeville on 4th June, but were pushed back to St Valery-en-Caux on the coast, from where they hoped to be evacuated.

Unfortunately on 12th June, a date imprinted on many Highland minds, the 51st Division were forced to surrender after two days of intense fighting, encircled by enemy troops.

The Seaforths suffered many casualties, the rest being taken prisoner and suffering a harrowing route march to a prisoner-of-war camp in Poland, Stalag XXB, where they remained until 1945 - though not before some had escaped.

A concert was held in Lochcarron to raise money for the ambulance fund run by the local GP, Dr Ferguson. The fund provided free transport to hospital by ambulance for those without the means to pay, while other patients were liable for half the expenses incurred.

Tighter controls were imposed on enemy aliens - citizens of enemy states resident in Britain. In consequence, five teachers at Gordonstoun School were interned along with a number of pupils, and ordered to give up all firearms in their possession.

The Stromeferry stationmaster, Mr Kennedy, was transferred to Burghead Station after 18 years. While at Stromeferry he had also been a coal and fish merchant.

Under emergency legislation, war factories now worked a seven-day week.

Up and down Wester Ross, various premises took on additional roles as First Aid Posts and ARP Posts (air raid precaution warden's posts). Kyle Hall, for example, and the Commercial Bank House at Dornie, served as both. Drumbuie Stores and the gamekeeper's house at Killilan were ARP Posts. Inverasdale Schoolhouse and Poolewe Nurses' House became First Aid Posts.

Home Guard Established

The *Ross-shire Journal* carried the following item on 17th May 1940.

Defence Volunteers for Ross-shire

Appeal for Recruits. The Lord Lieutenant of Ross and Cromarty, Sir Hector Mackenzie of Gairloch, has received a telegram from the Secretary of State for War asking him to assist and co-operate with the chief military authorities in the recruitment of Local Defence Volunteers.

Ex-officers and members of the British Legion and others aged 17 to 65 who had a knowledge of firearms, were asked to enrol at the nearest police station. At this stage the main requirement for the force was to keep watch for enemy parachutists. Later in the month, it was reported that 1,356 men had joined up in Ross-shire (then including Lewis). In August the L.D.V. were re-named the Home Guard at Winston Churchill's request.

From the summer of 1940 everyone was required to carry a National Identity Card and urged to carry a gas-mask.

On 14th June the Germans occupied Paris.

Over the summer, newspapers carried growing lists of casualties and missing men, as well as details of bravery awards, following the fall of France.

The age at which farm-work became a reserved occupation was lowered to 18. Any farmworkers presently in another job were required to return to agricultural work if they left that job.

In July, the minimum wage for farmworkers was increased. A ploughman, for example, if aged over 20, now received 51s. a week, up by 10s.6d.

On seven successive Saturdays from 15th June to the end of July, men born between 1906 and 1912 (aged 28-33) were required to enlist. The total number of men who enlisted at Dingwall during those weeks was over 300.

Dealing with Aliens

Dingwall Town Council debated in July how to deal with shopkeepers classified as 'enemy aliens'. Italy had declared war on Britain in June, so Italian-owned businesses like the local ice-cream shop were now affected.

One councillor complained that Italian-owned shops were flouting prescribed opening hours by opening on Sunday. At this time, shops were normally required to close by 6pm between Monday and Friday and by 7.30pm on Saturdays - although shops selling cigarettes and confections were allowed to remain open until 8pm, and there were no set hours for the selling of refreshments.

The Town Clerk agreed to warn all offenders, but called for flexibility.

If we had to comply with the law in all respects we would be in a bad way. We have to shut our eyes to some things.

From 3rd June, all aliens aged over 16 were required to be in their homes between 10.30pm and 6am. Unless authorised by police, no alien was to be in possession of a firearm, bicycle, car or boat.

1940 (continued)

Fishing ceased to be designated as a reserved occupation, so fishermen were now liable for conscription.

Under the National Milk Scheme, milk was supplied to mothers before and after childbirth and to children under five. Another scheme provided free milk to the poorest ten per cent of households.

Pupils of Killilan Public School in Kintail collected 40 dozen eggs which were sent to the Royal Northern Infirmary at Inverness. They also collected money to donate to the Services' Tobacco Fund.

'National butter' was produced from the start of July. 45 million new ration books were issued that month.

On 1st July, 15 people were killed when bombers attacked Wick.

Farmers in Wester Ross demanded that the wool price be revised.

Scottish Football League competitions were suspended for the war.

Wool Sales *(announcement)*

You can still send your wool to Brora for manufacture into blankets, tweeds, knitting wools etc. If your wool is under Government Control, a limited supply is allowed for manufacture.

T.M.Hunter Ltd, Sutherland Wool Mills, Brora.

Ross-shire Journal, August

Scrap Wanted *(announcement)*

Aluminium, brass, copper and old iron are urgently wanted for aeroplanes etc. Householders in Gairloch and district are asked to send any they may have - new or old aluminium - to their grocer. Mr Macdonald, Loch Maree Hotel, has very generously offered to collect and deliver same at Dingwall next week, free of charge.

Ross-shire Journal, July

Among cost-saving ideas of the time were experiments to make paper from potato shaws and petrol from bracken.

The *Ross-shire Journal* listed over 100 men currently missing in action. The Battle of Britain was fought out throughout the summer of 1940.

It was announced that Dingwall Academy would close for only five weeks' holidays in summer, but an extra fortnight would be given in the autumn from 20th September, to allow children to help with farm or croft work.

Controls on Offenders

There were strict penalties for those who transgressed war-time regulations. A man from Buchan was fined £5 after being reported by his own son for discussing military matters over the phone. In August, an Inverness man was fined £3 for having a light visible during the black-out. In September an Orkney man was fined £1 after his wife sent him tea and sugar without the authority of the Ministry of Food. Although there was currently a glut of potatoes, several traders were fined for selling them without a Control Order.

The Convener of Ross & Cromarty County Council, Major Stirling of Fairburn, appealed to householders to remove any items that might be a fire risk from lofts, and to hand in any items they did not need and which could be put to another use to help the war effort.

New cars could now only be purchased with a special licence.

Herring at Kyle sold for the maximum retail price, currently 98s. per cran.

Food Bulletin 5 *(announcement)*

This was one of a regular series of advertisements placed in newspapers by the Ministry of Food. The series would continue throughout the years of rationing and long after the war ended.

We should be using salads and vegetables all we can. And we should be making sure of our future supplies by sowing or planting every inch of our allotments and gardens. Perpetual spinach can be sown now for autumn and winter use, also carrots and late keeping turnips. Kale, savoy cabbage and sprouting broccoli can be planted now for winter and spring.

Ross-shire Journal, July

News from France

It was announced that Captain M.Maclennan, Seaforth Highlanders, who was from Plockton, had been killed in action. Between 1931 and 1938 he was headmaster at Achiltibuie Primary School. He had earlier been reported missing.

As the Battle of Britain continued in August, enemy planes lost over Britain since September 1939 totalled 289. Most had been shot down since 18th June.

At a meeting in August of the Wester Ross Local Ambulance Committee of the St Andrews Ambulance Association, the President, Lady Marjory Mackenzie, Gairloch, reported that the ambulance had turned out 130 times in 1939-40, covering 6,900 miles.

Despite the war, private hydro-electric generating companies continued to undertake new construction projects during 1940. Grampian Electricity Supply Co opened a 4-mile tunnel between two lochs near Dalwhinnie.

At occasional hearings of the North of Scotland Conscientious Objectors' Tribunal, most objections were rejected, but a few were accepted as valid.

Ross-shire Spitfire Fund

A fund was set up by the Lord Lieutenant for Ross-shire, Sir Hector Mackenzie of Gairloch, and Major John Stirling of Fairburn, Convener of the County Council, to raise £5,000 to pay for the building of a Spitfire. Similar funds were started elsewhere. In November the target was reached after an enormous response from the public.

Tributes were paid to George Ross, Ullapool, who had died at the age of 92. A retired general merchant, he had been largely responsible for founding the local Free Presbyterian Church in 1893.

By August, casualty totals among Ross-shire men in the Seaforth Highlanders had risen to 13 confirmed killed in action or died from wounds, 201 missing, and 76 confirmed Prisoners of War.

Branches of the Red Cross Society raised funds for Prisoners of War and the Seaforths Comforts Fund sent scarves, mitts and socks to POW's. Scrap iron and waste paper collected in Ullapool was sent south by boat and fetched the sum of £24 for the Ross & Cromarty POW Fund. In villages such as Applecross and Ullapool, penny-a-week collections were made on behalf of the Red Cross.

It was reported in September that the Ross-shire Deer Forest Association had made arrangements for sheep to graze on land previously used as deer forest. Meanwhile deer forest proprietors appealed to the Valuation Tribunal for a reduction in rates on their land - nobody was shooting, they pleaded, and therefore they had no income.

Mr Murray of Lochcarron Estate gave permission to men of the local Home Guard to shoot on his land, stipulating that the venison should be distributed locally to those who needed it.

A good start to the herring-fishing season was reported at Kyle and Ullapool in October.

Plans were made to poison rabbits which had been damaging crops. But with meat rationed, it was suggested they be shot for food instead.

Miss Campbell, a domestic science teacher from the Black Isle, gave a series of lectures in Lochalsh on war-time cookery. She praised pupils of Plockton School for providing the community with vegetables from their garden. On the same theme, a Utility Garden contest was organised in Lochalsh by Lady Matheson on behalf of the WRVS, to encourage more growing of vegetables.

Aultbea Transformed

The establishment of a naval base at Aultbea during the war, and the use of Loch Ewe as a gathering-point for convoys, transformed the village.

The Aultbea Hotel was requisitioned as staff quarters for fifty officers. Gairloch Hotel, 11 miles away, was also requisitioned as a naval hospital. Several hundred servicemen based at Aultbea were accommodated mostly in barracks, though some were billeted with local families.

A harbour boom was laid across Loch Ewe between Mellon Charles and Mellangaun. Five defence batteries were located around the loch. The buildings which housed the guns at Cove are still in place.

For the troops' leisure time, a cinema was erected at Aultbea - nowadays used as the village hall.

Army camps were also set up in nearby locations at Laide and Gairloch. During the war, various other buildings in Wester Ross were requisitioned, notably Duncraig Castle as another naval hospital.

Living with the War

Householders in certain areas were advised in October that they might be required to billet troops in winter. As there were several army bases as well as a naval base in the Aultbea district, families there were asked to help out.

Alice McLennan, who lived in Laide during the war, recalled how her family regularly had two men staying with them.

"It was like having people from another planet. These men's English accents, like their names, sounded very strange to us. However, several men later settled in the area."

Alice had to take her gas mask with her to school each day, and was told that, if there was an air raid, she should lie down in a drain. In the event, she did not witness either of two German air raids over Loch Ewe because they came at night and she was fast asleep.

Loss of *Port Napier*

Kyle harbour on 27th November 1940 was a busy scene as naval ratings completed their task of loading HMS *Port Napier* with mines brought from the east coast by rail. Almost a full complement of 550 mines had been loaded, along with 60,000 rounds of ammunition for the ships' guns, when suddenly a fire broke out below.

Frantic efforts were made to extinguish the fire, but to no avail. When eventually it was realised that the ship was likely to explode, and perhaps destroy the village of Kyle, a decision was made to tow her out to sea. She was taken into Loch na Beiste, a mile or so east of Kyleakin and safely away from human habitation, and abandoned. Later in the day the boat blew up and sank although, amazingly, most of the mines failed to detonate. In 1950, 526 mines were removed intact, with 16 being blown up on site.

In 1988, steel plates were salvaged from the *Port Napier* for their pre-atomic-bomb low levels of radiation.

Sales of vegetables enabled Plockton school pupils to raise some funds for a wireless set, which was presented to them by Lady Hamilton, Balmacara House, with her congratulations.

In October, a chaplain appealed for donations including a piano, wireless set and games, for a military hospital which was being established in Mid-Ross.

Ross and Cromarty Health Insurance Committee reported that nearly 20,000 persons in the county were now insured.

A whist drive and a dance were held in the Masonic Hall, Ullapool to raise money for black-out curtains for the village hall. A concert was held in Garve in aid of the Ross-shire Spitfire Fund.

At the annual autumn cattle sales at Aultbea, Poolewe and Gairloch, Messrs Reith & Anderson of Dingwall sold over 100 animals: milk cows, farrow cows, stirks and weaned calves.

It was announced in November that men aged 35-36 must register for service by the end of the year.

Hotels without Customers

The owners of the Gairloch Hotel, along with the tenants of Lochcarron Hotel and Cluanie Inn, wrote to the Licensing Court at Dingwall to say that they were doing practically no business because Ross-shire was now a restricted travel area. They asked whether it would be permissible to close their hotels or at least shut the accommodation while keeping a bar open. The Court replied that they had no powers over such decisions but stressed the public interest should be considered.

Achnashellach Whist & Voluntary Workers Club sent Christmas parcels at a cost of £1 each to eight local men serving with the forces.

Residents around Totaig complained to the County Council that the private ferry service across Loch Duich between Totaig and Dornie had ceased operating.

The Ministry of Transport ordered that the Kyle-Portree ferry service be withdrawn as a war-time economy, but also awarded grants covering almost the full cost of re-building the Garve-Ullapool and Stromeferry-Auchtertyre roads.

The War Continues

Anthrax Experiment

Gruinard Island was used to conduct experiments in biological weapons. Canisters of anthrax were fired from the mainland onto the island, killing its population of sheep.

In July four German bombers mounted an air raid on Loch Ewe. Fortunately there were only two ships lying off Aultbea at the time, and neither was hit. Local ack-ack units responded, and a dinghy was found in the loch later, raising hopes one of the planes had been hit.

Clothes rationing was introduced.

The Arctic Convoys

On 6th February, a fleet of ships made up convoy PQ-11 which sailed for Northern Russia from Loch Ewe. Over the next three years 19 convoys would sail from the loch, including 481 merchant ships carrying badly needed supplies and 100 naval escorts. The final convoy sailed on 30th December 1944. (The full story is told in Steve Chadwick's superb book *Loch Ewe During World War Two*.)

HMS *Nelson*, now repaired after being mined in Loch Ewe, was in secret trials of a 'human torpedo' code-named the *chariot*, being developed to attack the battleship *Tirpitz* in a Norwegian fjord. *Nelson* stood in as a target in trials under cover of darkness off Kylesku. The real mission narrowly failed.

The 51st Highland Division, which had been re-formed in 1940 after the St Valery-en-Caux disaster, went into action for the first time since then in North Africa, performing valiantly in the El Alamein victory in October. The Division was subsequently involved in the invasion of Sicily in 1943 and the Normandy landings.

Strome School closed, its pupil roll having fallen to eight.

The Hydro-Electric Development Act (1943) established the North of Scotland Hydro-Electric Board.

Frank Fraser Darling wrote a series of articles about crofting for the *Ross-shire Journal*. Living on Tanera Mor from 1938, he had restored part of the island's croft-land to cultivation, experiences he described in his book *Island Farm*.

In Feburary 1944 the American ship *William Welch* was wrecked off the coast south of Melvaig. Only 12 out of 74 men survived, despite valiant rescue efforts.

On 3rd September, John Mackenzie of Gairloch, serving in the Guards Armoured Division, became the first Allied soldier to enter Belgium since 1940.

Strathcanaird School closed. The children transferred to Ullapool School.

The Rural Water Supplies and Sewerage Act was passed. It would help the County Council provide piped water supplies to communities after the war.

Among the first troops to enter Berlin as the war neared its end was Driver M.A.Mackenzie from Kyle, of the 7th Armoured Division - the Desert Rats. Having taken part in many successful campaigns since North Africa in 1942, he told the *Ross-shire Journal* that his only regret was that the troops of the 51st Highland Division, who had shared in the same campaigns, were not there too.

Duncraig Castle was gifted to the County Council by Lady Hamilton with a condition that it be used for an educational purpose. The first students to attend Duncraig Castle College enrolled on domestic science courses.

Garve was cut off for several days by flooding. At the station, the water level rose a foot above platform height.

Germany surrendered on 8th May 1945.

On 13th June all fifteen crewmen aboard an American aircraft returning home at the end of the war in Europe were killed when the plane crashed just south of Gairloch.

During August, sales were held to raise money for a Welcome Home Fund for returning troops. Most troops were still overseas awaiting demobilisation. The war was still going on in the Far East.

Four County Councillors visited Applecross by boat in August to assess the case for a track round the north coast.

Japan surrendered on 14th August 1945.

Right: Aultbea Hall was built in the war for servicemen stationed locally

More Tributes Paid
Killed in the War

After the war, the names of those who had lost their lives were inscribed on the memorials erected following the 1914-18 war. The lists were smaller this time, but still represented a terrible loss for close-knit communities.

In Gairloch, eleven names were added to the memorial at the Crask. In Aultbea, eight names joined 34 previously inscribed. Another name was added at Dundonnell and one at Garve.

Lochbroom suffered heavily, the names of 23 men and one woman being added to the 58 who fell during the First World War. Four had served with the RAF, six with the Royal Navy, including a woman with the WRNS, and two with the Merchant Navy. Eleven men had fought with the Seaforth Highlanders.

Lochalsh lost 18 men, five with the Seaforths, while eight names were added to the Lochcarron memorial.

Two men from the Kinlochewe district were killed during the war, both serving with the Seaforths. Corporal D.Matheson was killed in earlier fighting during the retreat from France, and Private C.Tough as the Allies advanced into Holland in late 1944.

Left: Lochalsh War Memorial

Below: Nostie Bridge Power Station: the North of Scotland Hydro-Electric Board ensured that power stations were built to a high standard using local stone

Post-War: New Challenges

1946

Construction of the Cluanie Dam in Glenshiel was completed.

The government awarded a grant of 85% of the cost of a track round the north Applecross coast *(see 1945)*. Unfortunately the track, when built, was wide enough only for a motorcycle. It would not be until the 1970s that a proper road was made.

The Highlands & Islands Advisory Panel was set up to explore ways of improving prosperity in the Highlands. The panel, whose powers were limited (as the name suggests), reported direct to the Secretary of State for Scotland *(see 1965)*.

Passenger trains ceased to operate on the Strathpeffer branch railway. A local development association had recently taken over Strathpeffer Pavilion but could never recapture the village's former glory.

Lochalsh Estate, including Balmacara House, was bequeathed by Lady Hamilton to the National Trust for Scotland.

1947

Balmacara House was leased by the County Council from the National Trust for Scotland as a boys' agricultural training school. Until 1955, a head teacher was shared with Duncraig Castle College.

Tulloch Castle, Dingwall, was gifted to the County Council by Colonel Vickers, and re-opened as a hostel for west-coast girls attending Dingwall Academy.

The Territorial Army resumed recruiting. The 4th Battalion Seaforths were re-numbered as the 11th. The Lovat Scouts became a gunner unit with links to the Ross Mountain Battery.

1948

Work started on the Fannich hydro-electric scheme *(see 1950)*.

Agricultural Advisory Committees were set up under the Agriculture (Scotland) Act, one committee serving Ross-shire.

A single-manned veterinary service covering Gairloch, Lochbroom and Applecross was set up under the Highlands & Islands Veterinary Service Scheme.

Tolls on the Dornie Bridge were abolished when the Kyle-Invermoriston road was upgraded to trunk status.

The last land raid in Scotland was staged at Knoydart.

The National Health Service was set up.

British Railways absorbed the LMS.

1949

Nostie Bridge Hydro-Electric Power Station in Lochalsh was opened after a three-year construction project. Electricity generated by the power station was supplied as far north and west as Lochcarron and Applecross.

Forestry Commission reports showed it owned 800,000 acres in Scotland, an area equivalent to Wester Ross. 6,000 houses had been built for its employees.

The Nature Conservancy was established. Clothes rationing ended.

Great Progress

By the end of 1949, the North of Scotland Hydro-Electric Board had two major hydro-electric projects operating, nine under construction (including Fannich), and eight others authorised. The Board also operated or were constructing a further 11 diesel-electric stations including one at Aultbea which opened in 1950. There were also five steam-power stations, the most northerly at Inverness (on standby only).

During 1949, 62 Highland villages and over 18,000 consumers were connected to the national grid.

The West Highland School of Adventure, based at Hartfield House, Applecross, was one of the first in Scotland to offer outward-bound courses in the late 1940s. The school subsequently closed but in 1995 Hartfield House became a centre for training courses aimed at rehabilitating young offenders.

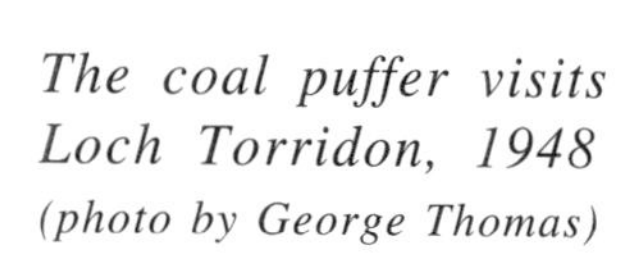

The coal puffer visits Loch Torridon, 1948
(photo by George Thomas)

Torridon in the Late 1940s

Crofting and Fishing

On the crofts around Alligin, sowing was done by hand in spring, using seaweed gathered in creels from the beach as fertiliser. For ploughing, the old handplough the *cas chrom*, or an ordinary spade, was used. There were no horses, and anyway the ground was too stony for a horse-plough.

A crofter expressed the hope that one day he and his friend would purchase between them a small motor-plough to replace the cas chrom, *which he likened to a relic of the Stone Age.*

Hay was cut by hand, women and men sharing the task. Sheep were clipped and their wool sent away to a factory which had to be nominated well in advance, as rationing and wool control were still in force. Crofters could buy back 40lbs of wool for knitting, at a reduced price.

In autumn, sheep bought at livestock sales were marked, and others brought off the hill for winter. Potatoes were lifted, and the women salted herring.

Fish was an important part of the weekly diet. The Alligin burn, which flows through the village, provided brown trout. Saith were abundant in the loch.

The saith come up in shoals to play on the surface. I have rowed through calm waters in the dusk when they were almost jumping into the boat.

While fishing one evening, the author and some friends landed near a cottage at Port Lair, south of Diabaig, with a message for the family who lived there, and whose only access was across open hill or by sea. They were welcomed and offered home-made cheese, bread and biscuits as the conversation flowed in Gaelic.

During 1948 Brenda Macrow lived at Inver Alligin. Later she wrote a popular account of her stay, Torridon Highlands. *The book describes a way of life at that time largely unchanged for generations.*

Village Life

Alligin School was still open in 1948, just along from the author's cottage. The ten pupils played happily near the shore during their breaks, and she enjoyed greeting them as they passed to and fro.

The boat-builder's shop was also open, while the Post Office doubled as a general stores, providing Miss Macrow with crockery on her arrival.

The local postman brought mail from Fasaig by bicycle, following the shore path and going as far as Wester Alligin. He also brought the weekly meat delivery from Inverness - meat was still rationed.

Film shows were presented every fortnight at Fasaig by the mobile cinema of the Highlands & Islands Film Guild. Dances and ceilidhs were welcome occasions.

The Sabbath was strictly observed, and its utter stillness struck the author.

Yesterday, I had watched children playing around the ruins of an old house in the village, and the air had been vibrant with their voices. Today, there was not a sound, not a soul in sight. There had been no service at the little kirk, for the minister went every third Sunday to Diabaig - but the day had begun in an atmosphere of solemn reverence which was never broken.

Comings and Goings

Locals ordered coal through the postmaster. Supplies were brought from Glasgow by a puffer twice a year. Most men in the village would row out to the boat to unload the coal, bringing it ashore and piling it in heaps from which villagers could then help themselves.

Another time a lorry was brought in from Fasaig aboard two motor-boats lashed together, to help with distributing the coal. Loads of any size, such as timber for an annexe to the youth hostel, were also brought in by boat.

People, too, came to Alligin by boat - the local doctor and nurse, for example, to give diphtheria injections to the children. There was a ferry between Alligin and Shieldaig, connecting with a mailbus there.

But getting around on the land was no easy matter. Alligin had no road and was reached by a path from the Diabaig road (itself just a gravel track) or the path from Corrie. Along the south shore of the loch, between Shieldaig, Balgy and Torridon, there was only a narrow track. The district nurse had her work cut out, for she covered the area extending eastwards from Balgy to Torridon, and from there to Diabaig.

Locals had appealed for years for a road to Alligin and were finally being heard: the Secretary of State for Scotland himself visited Torridon in 1948 to assess the need for new roads, later departing from Diabaig on a Fishery Board boat.

***Torridon Highlands* was published by Robert Hale, London, and ran to four editions. An earlier book by Brenda Macrow, *Kintail Scrapbook*, published in 1948, was an equally vivid account of her stay at Dornie.**

Tail-Piece

I RETURNED TO TORRIDON in 1985, and spent a memorable interlude renewing acquaintance with old friends and making new ones in the process.

Inevitably, some things had changed. Most of the homes now had television and what we have come to regard as the necessities of modern living. Plantations of Sitka spruce clothed parts of the glen. Fishing had largely become fish-farming, and access by road from the south had brought many visitors and tourists to this once-remote area.

Walkers and climbers of many nationalities stayed at the 80-bed youth hostel at the head of the loch. Inver Alligin village, now reached by a steep road near the gorge, was no longer isolated, and local people accommodated tourists and caravans during the holiday season. The cottage I occupied in 1948 had become a holiday home, with smart yellow paint and a sail-boat beached in the garden. Sheep still grazed on the short turf, and a single red-sailed boat, probably fishing for prawns, made a splash of colour on the sunlit loch.

Two things had not changed at all - the splendour of the terraced mountains and the traditional Highland hospitality. Everywhere I received an enthusiastic and heartwarming welcome. Having long given up driving, I had hired a bicycle from the garage at Kinlochewe, but soon found that I did not need it. Friends put their cars and time at my disposal, and took me anywhere I wanted to go.

Round the loch to Shieldaig, now given a rather exotic air by its 'snowdrop' street-lamps, and along the narrow coast road to the once-isolated village of Applecross, where we had a spectacular view of Skye, with the jagged peaks of the

Cuillin looming like dragons' teeth through smoky puffs of mist. Then over the Bealach na Ba, the ancient pass of the cattle, at the summit of which, over 2000 feet above sea-level, we were motoring through the clouds!

Loch Kishorn had been completely transformed by the construction of the Howard Doris fabrication yard which, though not a scenic attraction, gave much-needed employment to local people. Lochcarron had expanded considerably and had many modern shops including a fast-food takeaway.

Returning to Torridon, now owned by the National Trust for Scotland, with unrestricted access to the mountains, one felt that its popularity could only increase in future years.

Before leaving Torridon, I made a pilgrimage to the burial-ground at Annat, where the mortal dust of friends and neighbours who had gone on ahead had been laid to rest among their ancestors. In more recent years others have joined them but they remain vividly alive in my memory, as timeless as the unchanging Torridon hills, which still cast a spell upon the heart. *Brenda G.Macrow, 2002*

Brenda Macrow's cottage at Inver Alligin, 1948

Depopulation at Scoraig

A Case Study

In 1947 a booklet called *Scotland's Changing Population* was published by the Scottish Council of Social Service and drew attention to the problem of depopulation affecting Scoraig and other townships round Little Loch Broom.

The census of 1901 had recorded that the number of people living on the Scoraig peninsula, between Loch Broom and Little Loch Broom, was 140. Of those, 36 lived on the north shore at Achmore, and 104 people on the southern shore - 22 at Carnoch, 25 at Scoraig, and 57 at Lots of Scoraig.

In 1918 eleven families still lived at Achmore. But by 1934, in the space of just 16 years, the last inhabitants had left.

On the whole peninsula, the population had fallen to just 25 by 1947. There were only 9 women, 12 men and 4 children left. Three children attended the side-school.

In addition to crofting, six men fished for lobsters and salmon, one was the general merchant, one the postman, and one was paid by the County Council to look after the footpath to Badralloch. One of the women was the teacher at the side-school, and another man was a missionary.

The writer commented on the problems facing such a small and dwindling community without even a road.

In bad weather the mail may be days late. A steamer calls every ten days with goods, which can be handled only in good weather, as they have to be trans-shipped by small boat.

Without sufficient customers, the general merchant (Mr MacIver) could not run his shop indefinitely. Once he stopped, how would the people obtain supplies? Houses needed attention. There was, of course, no piped water or electricity.

At Badralloch ten families remained, but another seven had left since 1920. There was no shop or post office; but a merchant's van called fortnightly, and the township did have a road linking it to Dundonnell. It also had a side-school.

In 1918 eleven families still lived at Achmore. Sixteen years later the last inhabitants left.

Across Little Loch Broom, in the townships between Badluarach and Dundonnell, the population total of 152 seemed healthy enough and included 30 children. But even here, life was far from easy, and ten families had left since 1920. The report took local crofters to task for not making more use of once-productive land. Most crofters had a cow and some sheep but only used their land to grow a few potatoes. The report even criticised the authorities for allowing this to happen.

A crofter may be ejected if he fails to cultivate land properly, yet the Land Court rules that land under grass is not losing fertility, and hence the crofter who leaves his croft in grass is not cultivating the land improperly.

The population was elderly, the proportion aged over 65 being 20%, as against a national average of 9%.

Evacuation

The writer issued a stark warning:

Unless some drastic action is quickly taken to reverse the population trends in the crofter counties, the peninsular and western parts will be empty within a generation or two, for it is worth noting that in a small population there comes a time when any further depopulation makes it impossible for those who remain to carry on, and the place has to be evacuated.

Conversely, and cheeringly, a small addition to a small population can make a very big improvement in conditions. Indeed, a small emigration from the central belt of Scotland - and there are people ready to come if work and houses are available - would repopulate the Highlands.

New Settlers

Following this report, an attempt was made in 1949 to attract new settlers to take over untenanted crofts in Scoraig, but without lasting results. The move had the support of the landowner Sir Michael Peto and Glasgow-based Clan Albainn Society.

The last remaining families of the original Scoraig community abandoned their homes on the peninsula in the early 1960s, moving to Ullapool, Strathcarron and Dingwall.

However, another era was about to begin, as a new wave of settlers made homes on Scoraig from 1962 onwards, this time successfully *(see 1965)*. By 2000 the population had grown to a remarkable extent, with a number of second-generation inhabitants.

Into The Fifties

THE 1950s PROVED another tough decade. As the population continued to fall, several communities found themselves struggling to survive.

Still, at last there was some cause for optimism, with the construction of hydro-electric schemes giving both employment in the short-term and a vital improvement in the quality of life in the long term.

Piped water was provided to a number of areas for the first time during the late 1940s and 1950s. The standard of housing improved. The County Council built over 100 houses in Wester Ross in the first decade after the war. Few thatched or black houses remained occupied.

Halfway through the century, Church of Scotland ministers were invited to write reports about life in their parish for the *Third Statistical Account of Scotland.*

The Lochbroom minister reported a flourishing herring fishery at Ullapool, where the pier was being extended and twenty lorries operated locally.

The Gairloch minister, writing in 1953, lamented the decline in local crafts during the century. There were two blacksmiths in the parish, compared with seven in 1900. Boat-building ended in the 1930s.

Fishermen and lorry-owners had suffered recently when lorry-drivers could not get fish through to markets on the east coast due to poor roads and bad winters.

On a positive note, two small factories had been established: one at Firemore in 1952, assembling ploughs for export, another at Ceann an t-Sail (Gairloch Harbour) processing seaweed. Unfortunately they did not remain viable.

By the 1950s the population of Wester Ross had been falling for longer than anyone could remember - since 1861, in fact. In Applecross and Lochbroom, the population fell by over 50% between 1901 and 1951. In Gairloch and Lochcarron the drop was over 40%. In Lochcarron there were now only two primary schools open: Craig, a single-teacher school with 12 pupils, and Lochcarron, with 60 pupils taught by four teachers.

Only in Lochalsh, where Kyle had continued to develop, had the population begun to show an increase in recent years. Even so, the overall total in Lochalsh had fallen since 1901.

Population Trends

	1831	1851	1901	1931	1951
Glenshiel	715	573	343	317	310
Kintail	1240	1009	491	376	297
Lochalsh	2433	2299	1830	1525	1627
Lochcarron	2136	1612	1442	967	822
Applecross	2892	2709	1615	1034	735
Gairloch	4445	5186	3797	2376	1991
Lochbroom	4615	4813	3207	2004	1448
Total	18,476	18,201	12,725	8,599	7,230

Hydro-Electric: A New Era

Ross-shire Projects

The Conon Valley Scheme, begun in 1946 and completed in 1961, was the main Wester Ross hydro-electric project, and included several subsidiary operations. The first completed was Fannich in 1950, with Grudie Bridge Power Station, Lochluichart, generating 24 megawatts of power using water piped from Loch Fannich. The Glascarnoch project was completed in 1957, supplying Mossford Power Station at Lochluichart (24 mw) with water piped from Loch Vaich and Loch Glascarnoch.

A smaller run-of-river power station, Achanalt, opened in 1951 and generated 2.4 mw of electricity, while Luichart Power Station, built before the war, generated 34 mw. The overall scheme was completed with the power stations at Tor Achilty and Orrin. Conon Valley was just one of several major schemes in the Northern Highlands, the others including Shin, Affric, Cannich, Glen Strathfarrar, Beauly, Garry, and Moriston.

Three smaller hydro-electric power stations were built elsewhere in Wester Ross: **Nostie Bridge**, Lochalsh (1.25 mw); **Kerry Falls** near Gairloch (1.25 mw); and **Loch Dubh** near Ullapool (1.20 mw).

The Fannich Scheme under Construction

In early 1950, a group of reporters was invited to come and see work in progress on the North of Scotland Hydro-Electric Board's Fannich project. They were taken 160 feet down a shaft to view construction of the tunnel leading down from Loch Fannich to Grudie Bridge Power Station.

Some 700 men were employed on the tunnel, which was 3.75 miles long and 10 ft in diameter. Another 80 men were building the power station, and a further 15 worked on the pipeline.

The holing-through of the Fannich Tunnel was completed on 3rd March 1950, with an error of less than 2 inches. 150,000 tons of rock in total were excavated.

Workers at Fannich lived in a specially built camp, as was the case with all remote schemes. The Consulting Engineer for the project was the firm of Sir Alexander Gibb & Partners. The Gibb family had local connections, being proprietors of Gruinard Estate.

On 14th September, the tunnel was completed when the last section of rock between it and Loch Fannich was blown through. Temporary bulkheads initially prevented water from the loch from surging down to the power station at Grudie Bridge, until it was ready to begin generating electricity in mid-November.

Before that, a dramatic incident occurred on 11th November when a manhole-cover on the pipeline running down the hillside above the power station blew off, sending water soaring over the power house, tearing branches from trees and washing away 50 yards of road.

There was one fatal accident during construction at Fannich.

Hydro-electric construction work gave much-needed employment to Highlanders at a very difficult time. At Glen Affric, out of 1,739 men employed in January 1950, one third (562) were Highlanders. Most men were from other areas of Scotland, six per cent were Irish and four per cent English.

Left: Grudie Bridge Power Station

Right: A peaceful scene at Applecross

Left: Rushes take hold on crofting land near Melvaig

Diary of a Year

1950

Gairloch Lights Up

For the first time, 70 homes in Gairloch were provided with electricity when Mrs Maclean, wife of the proprietor of Aultbea, switched on power from the new Aultbea Generating Station of the North of Scotland Hydro-Electric Board.

It was the first stage in a programme which would connect 500 homes in Gairloch parish over the next year, with 83 miles of overhead distribution lines. Lines had already been erected from Aultbea as far as Charlestown, with consumers along the way due to be connected within weeks. The following year, a new hydro-electric power station opened at Kerry Falls near Gairloch.

A fuel depot was opened at Kyle by Scottish Oils and Shell-Mex Ltd. Kyle had recently been declared a special distribution area for petrol, paraffin and oil, with the effect that fuel could be bought at reduced 'North Zone' prices. Several other districts in the northern Highlands had already qualified for a similar entitlement.

House-Building

As the County Council Housing Department looked for ways of building new homes at a reasonable cost, a design using foreign timber was increasingly adopted. *Swedish houses* had already been built in a number of Wester Ross villages, including Gairloch and Ullapool; and a further twenty were approved that year for a site on the Plock of Kyle. When these were completed at the end of 1950, twenty more were ordered for the village, four for the families of employees of the Hydro-Electric Board. However, not everybody approved the design. John Macdonald, County Councillor for Applecross, complained about their alleged high maintenance costs.

Unusual Fishing Venture

The County Council objected to a proposal for a whaling station in the Minch herring-fishing area, arguing that blood from harpooned whales could pollute fishing grounds. At this time, sharks too were being commercially hunted, by Tex Geddes, based in Mallaig and Soay. He had worked with Gavin Maxwell out of Soay from 1946 until 1949, when Maxwell gave up.

Nature Reserves Not Wanted

Ross & Cromarty County Council's Planning Committee protested against a proposal by the Scottish Nature Conservancy to purchase land as Nature Reserves. Areas of Wester Ross earmarked for possible reserves included 'the top end of Loch Maree' and the Summer Isles. While noting that the Nature Conservancy had powers of compulsory purchase, the Council Convener urged that, if their aim was to protect wildlife, "they should not draw people's attention to it by forming reserves".

In 1951 the Nature Conservancy acquired Beinn Eighe and surrounding area for a Nature Reserve.

The County Council examined the case for developing either Gairloch or Badachro harbours (or both) as fishing ports. The Surveyor advised that the success of such development depended on the upgrading of local roads. Fishing markets had been lost lately due to roads being blocked for too long by snow. Noting this, the Council also decided to approach the Herring Industry Board to ask them to build fish-oil and fish-meal factories at Gairloch and Ullapool.

New Pier for Kyle

Construction of a fishery pier at Kyle was approved by the County Council.

Playing fields were built on land reclaimed from the sea at Pladaig, Kyle, at a cost of £16,000. Most of the funds for the project were raised by the local Playing Fields Association.

The Post Office announced that new telephone kiosks would be installed at Altandubh, Badachro and Toscaig. Such decisions were welcome for townships where many houses still had no phone.

Hydro Camp Dance

An enjoyable invitation flannel dance was held in the Balfour Club at Fannich Hydro-Electric Camp last Friday. These functions help lighten the sometimes arduous hours of duty for the people who are employed in a rather remote area.

Ross-shire Journal, June

A depot for the sale of crofters' handwoven tweeds and tartans was opened on Shore Street in Ullapool, under the auspices of Highland Home Industries Ltd.

It was reported that raids organised by gangs of poachers in deer forests in Wester Ross had decreased thanks to constant patrols by owners, keepers and stalkers.

The problem of organised poaching gangs taking salmon and trout from local rivers was also discussed in 1950.

A memorial was unveiled to men of the 51st Highland Division killed at St Valery-en-Caux in France in 1940.

Water Supply Wanted

John Macdonald, County Councillor for Applecross, urged that Ard-dhubh be given priority for a water scheme. Water currently had to be brought into the township by boat or collected from the gutters on cottage roofs. The community had no road either, but if forced to choose between having a new road and having piped water, said Mr Macdonald, the people would prefer water.

Drumrunie Hotel, ten miles north of Ullapool, burnt down.

A Sign of Things to Come

The Highland Development League noted that incomers on Mull were buying every cottage that came on the market, discouraging local couples from getting married as there was no affordable housing left.

Regret for Old Ways

In an editorial, the *Ross-shire Journal* lamented the gradual disappearance of the west coast crofter-fisherman.

In 1950 a made-to-measure suit cost £6 at Hepworths, Dingwall.

Protection Guaranteed

Scientists developed a cream which they claimed would ward off midges for up to 3 hours. The great news was announced by the 'Sub-Committee for Midge Control' of the Scottish Scientific Advisory Committee.

1950 (continued)

Among various annual events held in 1950 was a successful *Gairloch Highland Games* at Achtercairn. The *Ardelve and District Agricultural Show and Sheepdog Trials* at Conchra had judging categories including livestock and dairy produce, while the first *Kyle area music festival* was declared a great success.

Only Gaelic

The number of people in Scotland who spoke only Gaelic had fallen so low by 1950 as to make them worthy of occasional newspaper comment. They included Mrs Catherine Ferguson, aged 88, who lived in Ullapool but was originally from Harris.

The Education Committees of Ross & Cromarty and Sutherland County Councils, and An Comunn Gaidhealach, appointed a regional organiser to promote 'cultural, recreational and social activities suited to a Gaelic environment'.

400 Glasgow school pupils came to Ross-shire in October to help with potato-picking. They stayed at three camps including one at Brahan Castle.

On the Kyleakin Ferry
Good Days and Bad Days

A record number of vehicles (199) was carried on one day in late July 1950 by the three regular boats.

This does not sound much now, but involved some 100 crossings. It also compares well with 1917, when the service was operated by a rowing-boat and 40 cars were carried - in the year!

Good news was followed by bad. In August all three vessels were out of action during one of the busiest weekends of the year. Over 500 passengers were delayed. Debate over the boats' unreliability rumbled on for months before, in December, a new ferry, capable of carrying four cars plus passengers, was ordered.

The slipway at Kyle was reconstructed in the winter of 1950-51.

As if to emphasise the need for a reliable ferry, Kyle Fire Brigade were called to incidents on Skye such as a fire in July at Campbell's Temperance Hotel in Broadford. Time was of the essence, but before the fire crew could reach Broadford, that vital crossing to Kyleakin still had to be negotiated.

Mrs Sawyer of Inverewe Gardens donated the proceeds from the season's visits to the British Sailors' Society.

No Politics, We're Councillors

Already in 1950 devolution was topical. A million people signed a 'Scottish covenant' and a fourth meeting of the 'Scottish National Assembly' was held in April. Ross & Cromarty County Council sent a delegate to the Assembly, but only after a heated debate in which one councillor stated in support: "I do not want it to be known that this Council is not sympathetic to devolution. We want to have a say in our own affairs; we don't want to be dictated to from Whitehall." But Duncan Macrae, councillor for Dornie, argued that the County Council should "steer clear of politics".

The Scottish Farm Servants' section of the TGWU applied for an increase of six shillings a week in their minimum wage. The request was refused by the Scottish Agricultural Wages Board.

Roads and Transport

The County Road Surveyor reported on his survey of a possible road to Inver Alligin. A road was built in the mid-1950s.

W.D.Mackenzie, Garve, announced that their Achiltibuie-Ullapool bus service would operate only once a month from September. The same firm operated the thrice-weekly Ullapool-Inverness bus service.

The Kessock Ferry Joint Committee, whose members were drawn from Ross & Cromarty County Council and Inverness Town Council, ordered a new boat for the service, able to carry five cars and 100 passengers. The Committee also announced plans to re-construct the piers at North Kessock and South Kessock, to be ready for the boat's arrival in 1951.

In July, British Railways began offering cheap day and half-day excursions on the Kyle line.

It was announced that the Strathpeffer branch railway would close completely in 1951. Passenger trains had already ceased running in 1946; now goods traffic would end.

Not for Turning

A party of Swiss motorists got more than they bargained for when they tried to drive a car along the path round the North Applecross coast, mistaking it for a vehicle track. Their valiant attempt to reach Lonbain Youth Hostel was eventually brought to a halt at a 3-foot wide bridge where, finding they were unable to turn, they had no option but to get out and physically carry the car about.

Rationing: No End in Sight

Rationing was still in force at the start of the decade. A monthly round-up, *Rationing News,* was published in newspapers, with advice about such matters as availability of canned meats, sugar for making jam, and dried egg. A series of food bulletins started by the Government in 1940 *(see above)* was also still running. *Food Facts No.499* was published on 9th January, with advice to mothers on the benefits of giving cod liver oil and orange juice to babies.

Coal could only be obtained from a nominated coal merchant. Customers could only change their supplier on application to the Local Fuel Overseer.

Soap was de-rationed in 1950. The weekly meat allowance was varied, for example for corned beef, after Britain refused Argentina's demand for higher prices.

There were fixed maximum prices for various commodities including wool. During 1950 the Wool Marketing Board was established by Act of Parliament to take over the functions of the Wool Control Office. Wool was now included in the annual review of farm prices as a commodity entitled to an assured market and guaranteed price. All wool was to be sold *to* the Board, then re-sold *by* the Board at auction.

21st May marked the start of a new rationing year. The price of bacon was raised, while the existing system of points rationing which provided incentives to shoppers on selected items was scrapped.

Petrol rationing ended on 30th May after ten years. Suppliers raised the price of petrol to 3s. a gallon the next day. Until then, motorists had been allowed to drive 180 miles a month.

Strathpeffer: End of an Era

The contents of the main Pump Room at Strathpeffer Spa were sold off. They included glass mugs used for drinking the waters and "Madame Recamier" sofas.

During the summer, the pleasure-steamer *Lady Killarney* made regular calls at Kyle. A team from the village played cricket matches against the crew.

Problems in Winter

The County Road Surveyor reported severe disruption on the roads during wintry weather in December 1950. At the height of a storm which lasted for several days, 45 men were working to clear the Gairloch road and 30 on the Ullapool road. Ullapool had been cut off for two days. The surveyor put the blame for the chaos on fish lorries *(see below)* setting off in all weathers and blocking roads after getting stuck. He suggested that, in future, lorries form a convoy preceded by a snowplough.

At one stage, it had taken a squad of roadmen thirty hours to clear the Ullapool road to let an ambulance through.

Happy Days

Pupils of Poolewe School enjoyed a Christmas party in the village hall, with tea, songs, dances, sketches and games, a visit from Santa, gifts on the tree, and each child given a going-away present of a cracker, balloons, sweets and fruit.

In its final issue of 1950, the *Ross-shire Journal*, noting that Hogmanay was about to fall on the Sabbath, expressed regret that celebrations would not be held over till Monday, the custom in earlier years.

Chasing the Herring, 1950

Top Prices

Herring fishing in 1950 was still subject to price control. The current maximum per cran was £4 18s - but after controls were lifted, prices rose to as much as £7 or £8 depending on demand.

Catches varied greatly, week to week, from less than 20 crans per boat to more than 80. A cran represented some 1000 fish. The *Ross-shire Journal* reported on one week's landings in February:

"At Ullapool 35 boats landed 650 crans, mostly from 80s *(£4)* to control price. At Kyle, 3 boats landed 220 crans, with 150 sold to the home market, the balance for meal and oil."

Ullapool was now busier than Kyle, a reversal of the situation between the wars, and had a good season from January to March: 25,000 crans of herring fetching £80,000. The season lasted longer now, extending right through the summer.

Road Links

Gairloch was also an important port. Fishermen from Kintyre and Ayrshire generally landed there rather than at Ullapool or Kyle. Factors in the success of a landing harbour included the number of buyers based there but also its road connections and the ease with which fish could be transported to the main markets on the east coast. Gairloch, Kyle and Ullapool all suffered from sub-standard road links at this time. In 1950 the Herring Industry Board announced plans to focus support on one west-coast port only. Ross-shire MP John MacLeod risked the wrath of the Kyle and Gairloch men by asking the Secretary of State for Scotland to back Ullapool.

Kippering

A special effort was made at Ullapool harbour in the summer of 1950 to promote sales of kippers, mainly to the American market. From July, kippers were wrapped and packed in wooden boxes at the pier, ready for shipment.

The *Ross-shire Journal* reported on 28th July that, of 440 crans landed at Ullapool the previous week, over half had been bought for kippering.

Quotas

Just as there were controls on the price of herring, there were also quotas to limit catches. In August 1950 Ullapool reached its seasonal limit for cured (or salted) herring. The Herring Industry Board responded by announcing that, henceforth, herring landed at Ullapool for curing must be transported either to Wick or Buckie - herring for Buckie to be landed by 3pm, and for Wick by 1pm.

This red tape evidently did not find favour. Out of 560 crans landed the following week, 490 were sold for kippering and the rest for fish-meal.

Gutters

The success of the fishing at Ullapool encouraged several east-coast curing firms to bring staffs of gutters and packers, mostly women, to the village each year during the 1950s and '60s.

Urgent Need for Investment

A far-reaching White Paper entitled *A Programme of Highland Development* was published by the Government in June 1950. It included a number of proposals for halting the longstanding trend of depopulation in the seven crofting counties, recommending expenditure of over £37 million.

On house-building, county councils would be assisted to build 600 houses between 1950 and 1953, and the Scottish Special Housing Association a further 100-150 houses. On roads, funding would continue to be provided through the Crofting Counties Road Scheme. Further grants were to be given for water supply and drainage schemes; for harbour and pier improvements; for tourism ventures; and for forestry development, enabling over 500 men to go into permanent forestry work.

On becoming MP for Inverness at the General Election in 1950, Lord Malcolm Douglas-Hamilton called for "a really large sum of money for Highland development of all kinds, administered by a small executive based in the Highlands".

Such appeals were to be repeated many times in the 1950s. But it was not until 1965 that the Highlands & Islands Development Board was established.

Give Us Roads

Meanwhile the Highlands & Islands Advisory Panel urged the Secretary of State for Scotland to set up a special fund to improve Highland roads, and Ross & Cromarty County Council Convener, Major Stirling, commented that, without roads, public service improvements were little use. "Roads are first essentials and in this, the Highlands lags a hundred years behind the times."

The *Ross-shire Journal* repeated the cry in an editorial. "The most desperate need is for improved communications, especially in remote areas where small communities are slowly but surely disappearing through their lack."

Day of Destiny for Kay

On Christmas Day 1950, the Stone of Destiny was taken from Westminster Abbey to Scotland by three students and a teacher, Kay Matheson, who later lived and worked in Gairloch.

The Fifties

1951

Kerry Falls Power Station, south of Gairloch, and Achanalt Power Station, Lochluichart, were opened by the North of Scotland Hydro-Electric Board.

MacBrayne's weekly goods steamer service between Glasgow and Stornoway, which called at many west coast villages, was withdrawn. The only goods now being brought into the area by sea were occasional deliveries of coal by 'puffers'.

Beinn Eighe was declared Scotland's first National Nature Reserve in November. The Nature Conservancy had bought the land from Mrs Greig for £4000.

At the General Election, John MacLeod retained Ross-shire for the National Liberals, with Unionist support, in a straight contest with a Labour candidate.

The Bealach na Ba road between Applecross and Tornapress remained closed to vehicles from 6th December 1951 until 6th May 1952.

Inverewe Gardens were gifted to the National Trust for Scotland by Mairi Sawyer, daughter of Osgood Mackenzie. She died the following year.

Work on the Glascarnoch & Strathvaich hydro-electric scheme began in the autumn. Camps for workers were established at both locations. Realising that remote Aultguish Inn was ideally placed to deal with demand from construction workers during the project, the proprietor of Lochluichart Estate, Mr Loch, personally took over the Inn's licence and built an extension.

Two houses on Shore Street, Ullapool were converted to a hostel by the Scottish Youth Hostels Association.

Food Rationing Ends

Rationing of tea was lifted in 1952, of sugar and sweets in 1953, and all food rationing ended in 1954 when controls on meat were removed. Many celebrated by burning ration-books.

Ullapool School was downgraded from Higher Grade status to a Junior Secondary School. Children continuing their education after 2nd year now had to move to Dingwall Academy.

During a storm in January, 28 east-coast drifters were blown ashore in Loch Broom. The salvage operation was directed by local councillor Denis Cooper, who was later awarded the MBE.

There were record herring landings at Ullapool. At Gairloch, the local herring fleet numbered five boats, with ten fishing for cod (as noted by the minister).

The Highland Fund, a charitable organisation providing low-interest loans, was set up to encourage economic activity.

Great Day for Shieldaig

Residents of Shieldaig and district were provided with electricity for the first time via a ten-mile extension of high-tension lines from Kishorn. Outlying houses were connected, enabling local man John Mackenzie to buy an electric cooker from the Hydro-Electric Board's mobile showroom on the same day that power was switched on. He faced an awkward journey transporting it to his home a mile from the nearest road at the south end of Loch Damh.

Lochalsh House and its lands were bought by the National Trust for Scotland.

Lochluichart Station and two miles of railway line were re-built a little further north because the level of Loch Luichart was due to be raised by hydro-electric developments. As well as the old station, cottages at Mossford were submerged.

A dance in the hall at Strathvaich Workmen's Camp in March was enjoyed by 200 people, a buffet and bar being provided by staff from Aultguish Inn.

Tractors, Horses & Smiths

In 1954, in the four northern parishes of Lochbroom, Gairloch, Applecross and Lochcarron, the number of tractors in use was 52 and increasing, while the number of horses, currently 158, was steadily falling. Townships which did not own a tractor could borrow one from the Department of Agriculture through their Tractor Service. This had started as a war-time measure to enable crofters and farmers to plough and harvest when so many men were away with the forces. At its height it had provided 1300 vehicles. The scheme was discontinued in 1955.

The steady fall in the number of horses inevitably reduced the workload for the few remaining blacksmiths' businesses in Wester Ross. With the death in 1954 of blacksmith Finlay Murchison (known as Philip) at Lochcarron, the smithy there closed. He was the last in a long line of smiths, his father and grandfather (also called Finlay) having run the business earlier in the century.

The Earl of Lovelace set up a limited company, Ben Damph Estates Ltd, with himself and his sister as the only shareholders.

Eilean Donan Castle was opened to the public for the first time.

Ross & Cromarty County Council discussed building a Stromeferry bypass. The road was included in the next five-year plan *(see 1959)*.

The County Council's Education Committee inspected sites for a new secondary school for South-West Ross, at Plockton and at Kyle, eventually choosing Plockton. But it would take ten years for the school to be built.

Lochcarron Shinty Club won the Sutherland Cup (a junior trophy).

Seventeen passengers were injured when a tour bus crashed at Dundonnell.

The County Council agreed to build a new pier at Toscaig.

Residents of Diabaig and Alligin held a public meeting in December to discuss the need for road improvements. Appeals were sent to every organisation that might be able to help - the County Council, the District Councils of Gairloch and Lochcarron, the Crofters Commission and Scottish Tourist Board - as well as MP

John MacLeod, asking for support. The following year a side-road was built to Alligin from the Torridon-Diabaig road, replacing the previous path.

The Crofters Commission was established under the Crofters (Scotland) Act, with its head office in Inverness.

Applecross Progress

In recognition of the remoteness and "special needs" of Applecross, funding was awarded by the government to Ross and Cromarty County Council to enable the Roads Department to upgrade the Bealach na Ba road. On completion of the project, supervised by local foreman Donald Sutherland, a track which had been notoriously twisty and frequently impassable was replaced by a good-quality tarmac road with improved alignments.

For the first time in several years a ferry began operating between Kyle and Applecross, using the new pier at Toscaig. Secondary schoolchildren from Applecross would in later years use the MacBrayne's boat to travel from Toscaig to school in Plockton on Mondays and back home on Fridays.

Members of Kyle Children's Welfare Association expressed concern about the health of children attending the local school. During a recent cold spell the classroom temperature had not risen above 33 degrees for several hours, and the open fires in the school were described as quite inadequate. The headmaster had at one stage decided the cold was too intense to risk letting pupils continue with lessons, and ordered them outside to play and warm up. Construction of a new primary school at Kyle began in 1959.

Glascarnoch Dam was completed. At the opening ceremony in March, Provost MacRae of Dingwall lowered a 10-foot gate which prevented water from flowing out through the dam, thereby starting the formation of the five-mile long Glascarnoch reservoir. Three houses - Strathdirrie, Glascarnoch, and Wester Aultguish - were submerged. Mossford Power Station by Loch Luichart, part of the same scheme, came into use in May. Sandstone for the handsome new building had been quarried at Tain. Six new houses for hydro-electric staff were built nearby with stone quarried at Tarradale. Mossford was the fifth of six power stations in the Conon Valley Scheme. The last, Orrin, opened in 1959.

A public meeting in Torridon set up a committee to discuss the lack of electricity in the area with the local MP.

Permission was granted for the first time for off-licence sales at the general stores in Applecross, which, like a number of West Highland communities, had a tradition of being dry. Mr Thomson was proprietor of both the shop and the hotel.

A new boat, *Lochalsh*, began operating on the Kyle-Kyleakin ferry service.

New playing fields at Kyle were brought into use.

It was announced that the Seaforth Highlanders would amalgamate with the Queen's Own Cameron Highlanders in 1961, as the *Queen's Own Highlanders (Seaforths and Camerons).*

A village hall was built for the Kintail community at the head of Loch Duich by the owners of the estate, the National Trust for Scotland.

The Royal family came ashore from *Britannia* at Applecross in August to visit Major and Mrs Wills, owners of the estate. Mrs Wills was the Queen's cousin.

A limestone quarry opened at Rhidorroch, Ullapool. The operators, William Linn & Co, planned to ship 2000 tons of lime a week south by sea.

Kintail, Lochalsh and Glenshiel shinty clubs merged to form Kinlochshiel.

A new hostel for west-coast boys attending Dingwall Academy was opened.

Four people drowned when their car slipped from the ferry at Kyleakin.

The Red Deer (Scotland) Act came into force, setting up the Red Deer Commission and giving it effective powers to curb the problem of poaching carried out by townspeople in gangs, who would come into an area by night, turn spotlights on a herd and massacre as many deer as possible. Ironically, the first trial under the Act saw three Contin men fined for poaching on the Garve-Achnasheen road.

Kyle Golf Club was re-formed.

Inverewe Gardens had a record total of nearly 45,000 visitors during 1959. This compared with 700 in 1948. In 1969 the total would exceed 100,000.

Pressing Roads Matters, 1959

The owners of the Strome ferry, Messrs Cumming, negotiated a new timetable for the service with the County Council, and ordered a new six-car vessel, *Strome Castle*, for delivery in July 1959.

However, just days later a deputation from the Council met the Secretary of State for Scotland to argue the case for a new bypass road along the south shore of Loch Carron, which would make the ferry redundant. The Highways Committee subsequently sought a grant of £550,000 from the Scottish Office Home Department to construct the bypass road *(see 1960).*

The Council also asked for £335,000 for a road to link Torridon and Shieldaig, known as the Balgy gap.

In July the Secretary of State for Scotland approved plans to reconstruct the Aultbea-Braemore road at Gruinard.

The County Council's Road Surveyor reported that £6,000 was spent during 1959 on maintenance of the North Applecross footpath.

In December it was announced that £1 million would be spent in Ross-shire under the Crofters' Counties Roads Scheme during the next three years.

The County Council asked the BBC for an apology for a broadcast, *A Trip to Ullapool By Road*, claiming it had made disparaging remarks about the state of the road. The remarks possibly hit home, however - the road was re-aligned and widened in the early 1960s.

Above: The old Royal Hotel in Ullapool was extensively damaged by fire in 1960

Scenes from Scoraig

Right: A rare picture of the old church at Scoraig. It was built by voluntary labour, shortly after the Free Presbyterian movement was established in the 1890s. Sadly, the church was badly damaged by fire after the last of the old community left.

Left: Marie Wilson from Australia, whose great-grandmother Catherine Macgregor emigrated from Carnoch, Scoraig, a century ago, visits the ruin of the old family croft with Gregor Macdonald. She later described her feelings in a letter to the Campbell family, who were among the last of the old community to leave Scoraig in the '60s:

"I suppose the highlight for me (apart from meeting so many kinfolk) was the walk into Carnoch. Words could never express how I felt that day. Such awe, such joy, such sadness. Just breathing in all around me and remembering with love those gone before, who had lived and worked there. Harsh times and a harsh climate, but above all such wonderful faith and love for God and each other. It's a day I will remember and keep close within my heart."

Diary of a Year

1960

Rail Closures and Protests

A deputation representing local authorities in the Highlands met the Scottish area chairman of the British Transport Commission to discuss a threat to withdraw rail services and close a number of stations in the north. The closure programme had been drafted to save costs of just £40,000 per annum, which many councillors argued was a small saving given the importance of rail services as lifelines in remote areas. A similar delegation had already travelled to London in December 1959 to meet the Transport Minister Ernest Marples, but had been given short shrift by him; and in May a further deputation travelled to London, but to no avail. Main-line stations including Beauly and Muir of Ord closed in June, along with the Dornoch and Fortrose branches.

Ross & Cromarty County Council requested British Railways to delay the departure of the early morning Kyle-Inverness train by up to 40 minutes in the event that the Stornoway ferry should be running late.

New School Plans

South West Ross District Council discussed plans for a new Senior Secondary School to be built at Plockton.

600 men were currently employed at the Glen Strathfarrar and Beauly hydro-electric scheme, the main dam being built at Loch Monar. Raising the level of the loch would flood several houses at Pait, at its western end. The scheme was to link with the Cannich and Affric schemes.

Crofter Conflict

There was resentment among crofters when the Crofters Commission put forward proposals to encourage wide-scale amalgamations of crofts, with the aim of creating more viable units and improving efficiency - but with the inevitable effect of reducing the total number of crofters.

While accepting that it was not possible for a crofter to sustain himself and his family from 3 or 4 acres of land, most crofters regarded the proposals as an attack on the fundamental ethos of crofting: security of tenure. The original 1886 Crofters Act had guaranteed that people's houses and land could not be taken from them.

The Commission eventually backed down.

Transport Troubles

Heavy snow affected Wester Ross at the start of the year. On 15th February over a hundred motorists were unable to cross the Dirrie Mor to Ullapool and had to turn back to Aultguish, where the inn provided meals until a snowplough was at last able to escort a convoy through to the west coast in the late evening. The following week, an ambulance with an 8-year-old patient took six hours to cover the 22 miles from Ullapool to Aultguish, through drifts up to 15 feet deep on either side. On the same stretch, a breakdown vehicle and six fish lorries were stranded.

Applecross Problems

In 1960, townships on the North Applecross coast still had only a narrow path to link them to the outside world. The community were still largely dependent for supplies on a boat operated by the Department of Agriculture, which visited the district approximately every five weeks.

These visits were already less frequent than formerly. Ross & Cromarty County Council were concerned to learn in July that the Department of Agriculture were considering reducing their frequency still further.

* * *

John Macdonald, County Councillor for Applecross, highlighted the difficulties which faced people living on the north coast of the peninsula, where several townships were over 12 miles from the nearest road-end.

It had, he said, taken 12 hours for a man from Fearnbeg to be carried along the path and eventually reach hospital. Doctors already had discretion to call out a helicopter - he suggested that, in future, a helicopter be automatically called to cases in north Applecross.

Highland Home Industries Ltd signed an agreement with the Highland Fund *(see 1953)* to promote the production and sale of hand-knitted and woven goods in crofting areas.

A new fire station was opened at Kyle.

The National Farmers Union on Skye met the Roads Committee of Inverness-shire County Council to discuss ways of improving the Kyle-Kyleakin ferry service. The Union stressed the need to ensure the welfare of livestock, which routinely suffered as a result of long delays waiting for the ferry. The possibility of a 24-hour service was discussed.

Tourist Associations Set Up

The Scottish Tourist Board announced that 'modest initial grants' would be made available to local tourist associations prepared to adopt its model scheme for promoting tourism - which included the setting-up and management of tourist information centres.

The first tourist association in Ross-shire, the Easter Ross Seaboard Tourist Association, was formed that year. Three local associations were subsequently established in Wester Ross.

The Scottish Tourist Board was at this time improving amenities in three Highland villages - Newtonmore, Lairg and Bonar Bridge - as examples for other communities to follow.

Meanwhile the Highland Tourist Development Co Ltd was set up to assist projects which aimed to increase tourist accommodation, facilities and amenities. Loans were offered, with no capital repayments due until projects were operational and earning money.

Upholding the Law

On Foot or Bicycle

In his annual report for 1960, the Chief Constable of Ross & Cromarty reported that his force operated just two motor-cars, both Austin A99s. The police force had a strength of 76.

There had been 1,845 crimes and offences in the course of the year, an increase of more than 200 from 1959. But only 217 cases had not been cleared up. 450 road accidents had occurred, of which 300 involved injuries. However, there were only four deaths.

1960 (continued)

Pictures Please

South West Ross District Council protested to the BBC about the lack of television reception in the area.

A contract for a new independent television station serving the North of Scotland was awarded to Sir Alexander King, chairman of North of Scotland Television, later re-named Grampian. The station was broadcasting by the end of the year. Unfortunately, in South West Ross, as in many parts of Wester Ross at the time, reception remained very poor.

Problems for Firemen

In February the Royal Hotel, Ullapool was gutted by fire while new extensions were being built. Nine people escaped after the alarm was raised in the small hours by hotel manager Kenny MacLean. The fire was so serious that brigades from Dingwall and Inverness were called out to help. They faced atrocious weather on the way west, the Dingwall tender becoming stuck in snowdrifts near Aultguish and having to be pulled out by the Inverness unit.

Later in the year the Dingwall Fire Brigade were again in action on the west coast, at a fire at a cottage in Charlestown, Gairloch, a distance of nearly 60 miles from base. Local volunteers, and men from the Boom Defence Depot at Aultbea, also attended.

Inverpolly Estate was sold by the Earl of Cromartie to Mr Davies from Surrey, whose father, a coal magnate, already owned Coulin Estate. Ownership was then transferred to Polly Estates Ltd.

Strathburn House Opens

90 guests attended the opening of Strathburn House, a residential home for the elderly, at Strath, Gairloch in May. The home, built by the County Council, provided accommodation for 21 residents in 13 bedrooms which were a mixture of four-bedded, two-bedded and singles. Miss M.Nicholson was the first Matron.

After the opening ceremony, guests adjourned for lunch to the Gairloch Hotel, where local-born piper Alex Macrae entertained them after travelling from Blair Atholl especially for the occasion. Strathburn House was the 100th home for the elderly to be opened in Scotland.

School Closures

The Education Committee of the County Council met in March to discuss whether or not certain schools should be closed due to falling pupil numbers and other factors. It was decided that *Badachro School* would close immediately, with children to transfer either to Opinan School or Achtercairn School. The school building had been condemned as sub-standard. However, its closure was later deferred by a year.

The committee also decided to close *Melvaig School*, with the children to transfer to Achtercairn School. It was noted that there would only be two children of school age in the Melvaig district by 1961, and none aged under five.

Ardindrean School, Lochbroom, was also recommended for closure. There would only be four children of school age in the district by 1961, with three under-fives. The children would transfer to Ullapool School. The decision to close Ardindrean was subsequently deferred for one year. The Committee, however, offered better news to parents in the Achnashellach district by deciding to keep *Craig School* open. It was noted that prospective forestry developments might bring families into the area.

Stromeferry Bypass

At a meeting of the Highways Committee of the County Council, Mr Macrae, councillor for Kyle, raised an issue which was to recur throughout the decade - and had already been discussed for many years.

This was the problem of delays to road-users caused by the ferry crossing at Strome on Loch Carron, and the need for a bypass road along the south shore of the loch.

"Whatever happens," he said, "the Council will have to face another three years of pandemonium at Stromeferry. From that point of view, they should press on as quickly as possible, in obtaining approval and grant for a road scheme."

When the possibility of collecting tolls to pay for the road was mooted, there were no objections among councillors - if that was what it took to get it built, then so be it. The Highways Committee recommended "that the Council take all possible steps to obtain a grant of at least 75% from the Secretary of State for Scotland towards the cost of the road, making it quite clear that if a grant was not forthcoming they would build the road themselves and recoup the expenditure by means of tolls."

In June, the Secretary of State for Scotland announced that he could not offer any hope of funding the bypass road in the near future *(see 1965).*

On Which Subject...

At a dinner of the Gaelic Society of Inverness, Professor Angus Matheson made a plea for the survival of small local schools. Their closure, he argued, was a death-knell to communities they served.

Illegal Trawling

Local MP John MacLeod was given an assurance by the Secretary of State for Scotland that fishery cruisers would patrol regularly to prevent illegal trawling in Loch Gairloch.

The re-building of four miles of the Ullapool-Ledmore road was approved at a cost of £35,000 per mile, funded by the Crofter Counties Roads programme.

Traffic Commissioners meeting in Inverness authorised new summer bus tour services from Ullapool, to be operated by Newton & Mackay, who had recently taken over from G.&A.Ross.

A proposed hydro-electric scheme at Fionn Loch and Lochan Fada fell foul of objections from the National Trust for Scotland and others on the grounds of possible damage to the environment. The project was refused consent by the Secretary of State for Scotland. Other applications by the Board, including the damming of Glen Nevis as part of a new hydro-electric scheme there, were also rejected on conservation grounds.

Mackenzie Chieftainship

The Clan Mackenzie Society was formed in 1960. It was an appropriate time, as the Lord Lyon King of Arms was in the process of arbitrating over claims to the right to be declared as the chief of the clan. Viscount Tarbat, son of the Earl of Cromartie, Castle Leod, Strathpeffer, succeeded in his claim. He also inherited the earldom on his father's death two years later. His son John is presently the sixth Earl and Clan Chief.

Inver Alligin pier was reported to be in need of repair. The visiting 'puffer' currently needed three tides in order to unload its cargo directly onto the shore. The County Surveyor arranged to meet the local boatbuilder to look at the pier.

Kyle Improvements

A fourth boat, *Kyleakin*, joined *Lochalsh*, *Broadford* and *Portree* on the Kyle-Kyleakin ferry service. The new vessel carried six cars. Meanwhile a new road bridge was constructed across the railway at Kyle, and a car-park built by the ferry slipway.

Fishing

Ullapool was a busy herring port in 1960, with many east-coast boats landing at the pier. Crews were taken home each weekend by a fleet of over 20 buses.

Tragic Accident

The Gairloch community suffered a devastating loss when four well-known local men drowned while on a fishing trip. They were the local GP, Dr Hugh Munro Flett, Wester Ross veterinary officer Robin Campbell, garage proprietor Mr Aonghais Macdonald, and newsagent and grocer Mr Roderick John Macintyre. Two men survived.

Another Matheson Link Lost

General Sir Torquhil and Lady Matheson sold their long-time home in Lochalsh, Duirinish Lodge, but kept a house in the village nearby.

The BBC filmed a programme in Inverasdale for their documentary series *Special Enquiry*.

Regimental Honour

To honour its centenary, the Ross Mountain Battery was officially awarded the Freedom of Stornoway by the Town Council. The Battery had links with both Stornoway and Lochcarron, its former HQ where volunteers had formed the *1st Company Ross-shire Artillery Volunteers* shortly after the Stornoway unit was set up. The name was changed to the Ross Mountain Battery in 1908, when the link with Stornoway was formed. Soldiers wore the Lovat bonnet and badge. In 1960 the Battery, still a gunner unit, had a volunteer strength over 500, with 60 at the Glasgow REME workshop.

An Ullapool-Stornoway Ferry?

Ross & Cromarty County Council asked the Department of Agriculture & Fisheries to support an Ullapool-Stornoway ferry service and sought funding towards the cost of a £500,000 ship for a Stornoway firm to operate the service. In December, the Planning Committee had a lengthy debate about the future of the Minch ferry and acknowledged that there might not be enough traffic to sustain both Kyle-Stornoway and Ullapool-Stornoway services *(see 1970)*.

The access track at the north end of Shieldaig known as Mary's Street, leading to three houses, had virtually disappeared through erosion by 1960. Lochcarron District Council asked the County Council to build a protective sea-wall.

Fare Increases

An application by Highland Omnibuses Ltd to increase fares throughout the Northern Highlands was rejected by Traffic Commissioners meeting at Inverness. On behalf of the seven local authorities concerned, it was argued that the application was ill-timed in the light of the closure in June of 24 railway stations north of Inverness. However, the Commissioners changed their minds in November, when fares were raised.

New Road Approved at Last

The Scottish Office awarded a grant for the building of the 'Balgy Gap' road between Torridon and Shieldaig. The consulting engineers announced that work would begin shortly and should be completed by 1963.

Foot-and-Mouth Scare

There was an outbreak of foot-and-mouth disease at the end of 1960. By late December, 94 cases had been notified in Scotland, most of them in Aberdeenshire, with 249 cases in Britain as a whole.

Last Words on his Subject

When Duncan MacPherson published his 34th and final yearly guide to Lochalsh and Skye, the Sunday Times publicised it - and he received a stream of fan mail from all over the world.

The Scottish Office installed a first computer in the Department of Agriculture & Fisheries, at a cost of £45,000, estimating it would save taxpayers £250,000 over a decade.

New Water Supply

A piped water supply was provided in the Inverasdale district. The main reservoir was Loch an Iasgair, with another smaller reservoir lower down. The supply was subsequently extended to Naast and Cove, using a subsidiary reservoir.

Gairloch District Council discussed the feasibility of buying Gairloch harbour from David MacBrayne Ltd. The company had asked £22,000, but an estimated £92,000 of expenditure was also required, which was too much for the Council.

A fishing-boat became stranded on rocks near Gairloch in October, and the Badachro life-saving company was called out. An anti-submarine frigate and fishery cruiser stood by, but the stricken vessel was able to re-float at high tide.

A new life-saving company was formed at Loch Ewe with a membership of 18 men. Equipment for the company included line-throwing rockets, a searchlight, and a 1500 foot whip.

Sea-Wall for Ullapool

The County Surveyor reported plans for a new sea-wall along the front at Ullapool, with Shore Street to be widened.

Diesels operated on the Kyle line for the first time in December, hauling goods trains. They also operated the Inverness-Aberdeen route for the first time in 1960.

The satellite *Echo* was visible in the night sky from South West Ross.

Long Service in Kinlochewe

The death was reported of Alexander MacIver, blacksmith at Kinlochewe for nearly 60 years from 1900 until his recent retirement. He was one of the last blacksmiths in Wester Ross.

Miss M.C.Mackenzie also retired after 47 years as the sub-postmistress at Kinlochewe. She had taken over in 1913 from her parents, who had themselves run the office since 1880 - the year in which a telegraph office was first opened in the village. The first telephone switchboard had been installed in 1938, converted to automatic operation only in April 1960.

Miss Mackenzie's sister Jean had worked beside her for the last 43 years. And their brother Roderick had been the local postman from 1919 to 1958.

The Sixties

1961

The primary schools at Alligin and Badachro closed.

In the national census of 1961, Lochcarron was one of only two parishes in mainland Scotland categorised as bilingual, with more than one in twelve children speaking Gaelic as their first language. The census recorded that over 1,000 people in Scotland spoke only Gaelic - no English.

Mr Macrae of Totaig Ferry advised the County Council in April that he had carried ten passengers during the winter. His request for the service to operate on a seasonal basis in future was approved.

An Inverasdale man was killed by a rockfall during construction of the tunnel at the Glen Strathfarrar hydro-electric scheme. It was the third fatality since construction work began in 1960.

Braemore House near Ullapool was demolished. The building, built in 1866 by Sir John Fowler, engineer of the Forth Bridge, had been accepted by the Scottish Youth Hostels Association from estate proprietor Mr Calder in the late 1950s but its upkeep had proved prohibitive.

The Fain road between Braemore and Dundonnell was upgraded.

Tourism Developments

New Holiday Centre

The owners of the 10,000-acre estate of Sand, four miles west of Gairloch, sought planning permission in 1961 for their Sands Holiday Centre complex. It was to include caravans and camping pitches with visitors able to enjoy sandy beaches, walks, and fishing in loch and river. Although there had been a campsite at Sand before the war, this was still a major development. The estate's new owners were Mr & Mrs Mitchell, Hertfordshire.

Luxury Hotel

The Earl of Lovelace also launched a tourist venture that year, becoming one of two shareholders in Loch Torridon Hotel Ltd, which he set up to manage his former home, Ben Damph House, as a luxury hotel.

With the completion of the Monar dam, the level of Loch Monar was raised. Some of the most remote houses in Kintail, at the loch's western end, were flooded.

Gairloch fishermen continued to discuss purchasing the pier from MacBrayne's *(see 1960)* but decided against it unless the Herring Producers' Association gave an undertaking to support the harbour.

Kinlochshiel Shinty Club won the Sutherland Cup at Fort William.

A recreation park and tennis courts were laid out on Quay Street by Ullapool & Lochbroom Tourist Association, who also opened an information bureau.

The opening of the new nine-mile road link between Torridon and Shieldaig - the 'Balgy gap' - was a long-awaited improvement to the area's road network.

The school at Opinan, between Gairloch and Red Point, closed.

MacBrayne's Ltd began carrying cars on ferries including *Loch Seaforth*. Vehicles were lifted on and off the boat in a side-hoist, up to six at a time. Kyle was one of the busiest ports on the west coast in these years, with *Loch Seaforth* on the Stornoway/Mallaig route, *Loch Arkaig* on the Portree service, *Loch Toscaig* sailing to Applecross, and local services to Kyleakin and Glenelg.

Dance Nights

Aultbea Village Hall was the focus of a thriving social life in the early 1960s.

Built out of a Nissen hut by the Royal Navy, it is complete in every detail with a large stage, tea-room and cloak-rooms. It is capable of seating hundreds of people, and the weekly dances there are widely known and patronised. Often a small BBC orchestra comes through to officiate.

(From *And It Came to Pass*, Barker Johnson)

1965

Plockton High School was formally opened in September by Judith Hart, Under Secretary of State for Scotland. People in South-West Ross had waited years for the new school but could count themselves fortunate in that, throughout the century, local children had continued to receive a full secondary education in their own area rather than travelling to Dingwall Academy *(see 1968)*.

The first meeting of the Highlands & Islands Development Board was held in November, and the final meeting of its fore-runner, the Highland Panel, in June.

Ross & Cromarty County Council held talks with the Scottish Development Department over a Stromeferry bypass road and North Applecross coast road. The Secretary of State for Scotland approved a Stromeferry road in October.

Kyle-Kyleakin ferries operated on Sundays for the first time in many years.

Ullapool staged the European Sea-Angling Championships.

Miss Mackenzie, proprietor of Garve Hotel, sold her transport firm W.D.Mackenzie Ltd. Four generations of her family had run the firm, which operated services including the Garve-Ullapool bus (originally horse-drawn).

A mobile library service started operating in Wester Ross.

The County Council diverted funds from road works on Lewis to upgrade the Garve-Ullapool road, angering islanders.

Scoraig Re-Settled

By 1965, five families had re-settled abandoned crofts in the township of Scoraig. Among the new settlers was a sufficient number of children to enable the primary school to re-open. The re-settlement of the peninsula was encouraged by landowners the Roger Brothers of Dundonnell Estate, and has since continued, with the population numbering around 90 by the year 2000; by then a secondary school was also open. The new Scoraig community pioneered the use of windmills for generating electricity to houses.

The Strome ferry crossed Loch Carron until 1970, when the by-pass along the south shore of the loch opened. Tom Patey recalled in One Man's Mountains *that waits for the boat could be lengthy.*

"Here, according to the tourist brochure, time stands still: so do long queues of irate motorists lining the roads on either side of the ferry. In the height of the tourist season there is more hot air vented at this remote spot than at many a Rangers-Celtic football match. The ferrymen belong to a different category. They stand aloof from the mob, performing their tasks with the unruffled calm and natural dignity of the Celt. Nothing short of an H-bomb could shake their composure."

A new County Council headquarters in Dingwall was opened by Willie Ross, Secretary of State for Scotland.

The North of Scotland Hydro-Electric Board failed in a fresh application for a scheme at Fionn Loch and Lochan Fada south of Gairloch. The plan was vetoed by the Secretary of State for Scotland.

1966-7

NATO built an oil storage depot and pier at Aultbea in 1966, then employing some 30 people, nowadays about 15.

Plockton airstrip was laid out in 1967. Loganair flights from Stornoway to Glasgow called daily at first.

The worst foot-and-mouth outbreak in Britain since 1923-24 resulted in the culling of millions of animals. The outbreak continued well into 1968.

1968

Plockton High School opened a hostel for children from outlying districts. A majority of parents in Applecross, Shieldaig and Lochcarron, whose children currently attended Dingwall Academy and stayed in the hostels there, requested they transfer to Plockton. From 1970, Lochcarron children travelled daily to Plockton on the new Stromeferry bypass; construction of that road started in February 1968. The Plockton Hostel thereafter accommodated mainly children from Glenelg and Applecross.

Eilean Ban, the small uninhabited island lying between Kyle and Kyleakin, was bought by local naturalist and author Gavin Maxwell with a view to living in the lighthouse and establishing a wildlife park. His death in 1969 prevented the realisation of the plan (*see 2000*).

1969

Most bus and ferry transport services in Scotland were nationalised under the management of the Scottish Transport Group, including the west-coast operations of David MacBrayne Ltd.

The Kyle railway line was closed by two landslips caused by blasting on the adjacent Stromeferry bypass project. For six weeks in summer, services began and ended at Strathcarron after a landslip near Attadale. A second, more serious rockfall in November buried a 200 feet-long section of the track and caused the line's closure until March 1970.

The Gairloch Conservation Unit was established, bringing together staff of local estates to co-ordinate a programme for assessing numbers of red deer and how many to cull. It became the first of many Deer Management Groups in Scotland.

Fearnmore, Applecross. This photograph was taken in the mid-1970s, when the township was still roadless and depended on a narrow track, wide enough only for a motorcycle. The only other means of access was a boat.

Life in Gairloch

Isabel Mackenzie reflects on life and change in her native parish

Isabel Mackenzie's house overlooks one of the finest views in Wester Ross, across Loch Gairloch to Badachro and the Torridon hills. Here on a croft at Strath she grew up and spent much of her adult life. Now retired from teaching, she keeps busy providing B&B for many visitors between spring and autumn.

Until the age of two, Isabel spoke English but her parents decided that, if she did not learn Gaelic soon, it would be too late. From then on, it was all Gaelic in the house until she went to school. Her mother came from Applecross, with relations at Shieldaig too. Her father was a native of Gairloch, her paternal grandmother from North Uist. Isabel thinks her Gaelic must include some dialect from all these places!

While she was still at primary school, war broke out.

"The Gairloch Hotel was converted as a hospital. There were barriers at Achtercairn and Achnasheen where permits had to be shown. There was a camp of Indian soldiers at Tollie, and a REME camp in Gairloch. Men from British Honduras and Newfoundland came to Kinlochewe to cut timber."

Rationing meant improvising. Isabel remembers loaves being made in tins of dried milk. Her father started a vegetable garden as part of the 'dig for victory' effort.

Achtercairn School was only a junior secondary in those days, so to continue her education after the age of 12 Isabel had to move to Dingwall Academy. She won a bursary, which made it possible to go - not all children could. At Dingwall she stayed in a hostel. "But there was no hostel for boys. They stayed in digs and bought their own food, which their landlady cooked for them."

Isabel was away from home for the whole of each term. "It just wasn't possible to come back, transport being what it was then and petrol rationed. Lochcarron children could take the train, but not us. I came home for just one holiday weekend."

She and her friends used to go the railway station in Dingwall every Saturday to meet any friends and relations passing through. She also saw her father when he came down to Dingwall on market day.

Teaching

Isabel enjoyed her time at Dingwall. Afterwards she went to university in Glasgow to study English and History, before qualifying as a teacher. Her first teaching post was at a secondary school in Kinross, but then she had a chance to return home as a primary teacher at Achtercairn, and took it. She was to remain at the school until retiring in 1991.

In her first years back at Achtercairn, the school had just three teachers. Isabel taught the first four years, Mrs Ross had years 5-7, and Mr MacLeod was in charge of the junior secondary years. There were also visiting teachers of sewing, art and music. The number of pupils at the time was about 50. There were other local schools at Opinan, Badachro, Sand and Melvaig - all closed by the 1960s.

Isabel Mackenzie and crofter Willie MacKintosh by the barn next to her house

In the 1970s, Neil Wilkie arrived at Achtercairn as headmaster. He made a great contribution over the next 25 years, during which time the school was upgraded to six-year secondary status. Isabel and her colleagues welcomed these changes, and others such as the provision of nursery education and playgroups.

"It is good for children to mix as early as possible. It could be quite daunting for children from isolated communities in the old days, when they suddenly moved to a bigger school." Isabel points out that education is now a major source of employment in Gairloch.

Changes

Looking back on changes in the local way of life, Isabel recalled how, during her childhood, her parents, like all crofters, used a horse and cart to work the land.

"One of my father's innovations after the war was to buy an old army lorry which replaced the horse and cart. A few children learned to drive on that lorry!"

Her father died in the mid-1960s, and now a neighbour, Willie MacKintosh, uses the croft to graze cattle and sheep.

As everywhere, Gairloch has seen changes as years go by. Church-going has fallen away, though several churches are well attended, and communion seasons are not the major events that they were.

"People came to the communions in June and October from as far away as Applecross and Raasay, some for four days, from Thursday to Monday. They were accommodated in houses all round. People from here also travelled to other communions, especially Shieldaig."

Isabel is keen to preserve local history and has been involved in several projects with Gairloch Heritage Museum, for example about schools in the parish. She was a member of the former Gairloch District Council and has been a Community Councillor for many years and is the present treasurer. The Great Wilderness Challenge is another enthusiasm. She participates each year, and praises the event's selfless organisers.

Isabel reflected on changes in tourism. "Just before the war, tourism was a growing industry. Visitors usually stayed a month in self-catering accommodation, with the father dropping the family off and coming back later. There were shooting lodges too, and a campsite at Sand. But the season was much shorter."

Indeeed, visitors can come to Gairloch at any time of year now, to enjoy some of the finest scenery and hospitality in the Highlands.

The decade saw great improvements in the transport network, as illustrated by the number of new roads opened in 1970. For the first time in over a century, the population rose slightly. Industry provided thousands of jobs at Kishorn after 1975. The BUTEC operation was established at Kyle. Fish-farming became widespread, and the 'klondyking' era began in Loch Broom. Shellfish was now the main target for local boats, and a seafood-processing factory was set up at Kyle. Visitor numbers rose and new hotels were built. Crofters were given the right to buy their crofts.

The Seventies

Diary of a Year

1970

Railway Re-opens

As the new year came in, the Inverness-Kyle railway remained closed between Strathcarron and Stromeferry as the result of a rockfall in November 1969 caused by construction work on the Stromeferry bypass road. It was decided in January that the line would not be re-opened until a protective shelter had been built across both it and the new road, as a safeguard against possible further rockfalls - and at a cost of £100,000. Meantime train passengers continued to be transported between Strathcarron Station and North Strome by bus and across Loch Carron by the ferry.

On 16th March, British Rail resumed running trains between Strathcarron and Stromeferry. Initially, train drivers were required to stop on approach to the rockfall zone until the resident roadworks engineer confirmed it was safe to continue.

The Scottish Rail Development Association, meeting in January, discussed the Kyle railway and declared it had an important future "whether or not the Stornoway ferry moved to Ullapool" *(see p.67)*.

Kyle Golf Course was re-opened after several years of restoration by members.

Vital Boat Service at Risk

To the concern of communities in North Applecross, the Scottish Development Department announced that funding was to be withdrawn from the Loch Torridon Transport Service. This vital lifeline had, since the First World War, provided the remote and roadless communities of North Applecross with a regular delivery of groceries and necessities. The cue for the Department's decision was the imminent retirement of the regular boatman; it had been decided not to seek a replacement.

Mind that Cow

John MacDonald, Ardarroch, created interest by deciding to paint his cows with a reflective liquid, to help motorists avoid them at night.

Kenmore Road Opens

A new road between Shieldaig and Kenmore was officially opened by Princess Margaret in May. The six-mile road was the first section of the long awaited North Applecross coast route. The Highlands & Islands Development Board pressed the Secretary of State for Scotland to approve construction of further sections of this road as quickly as possible. He obliged within weeks by approving a grant of 75% from the Scottish Development Department towards the cost of a further six miles of road from Kenmore to Cuaig, the balance to be met by the County Council and the HIDB.

Kyle-Balmacara Road Opens

A new direct road between Kyle and Balmacara was officially opened in April, further reducing journey times for drivers on the A87. The former route was via Badicaul and Balmacara Square.

A contract to build a causeway over Loch Duich near Morvich was awarded. This was the last section in the local re-development of the A87, following the by-passing of Carr Brae in recent years.

Now Showing

In 1970 Dingwall Picture House showed films only three evenings a week. On other nights the building was used as a bingo club. In January the film of Gavin Maxwell's *Ring of Bright Water*, with Virginia McKenna, was showing.

A 12-mile section of the A832 Kinlochewe-Gairloch road alongside Loch Maree was upgraded.

Ross and Cromarty County Council objected to a Ministry of Transport plan to allow lorries up to 44 tons on roads.

Plea to Fishermen

The County Council wrote to fishing interests urging them to use the Fishery Pier at Kyle, which had seen little use since its construction some years before. The Council drew the attention of producers and fishermen to recent improvements in all-important transport connections via the new A87 route.

Gairloch Community Association urged the County Council to invest in new facilities at Gairloch Harbour, which the Council had acquired from David MacBrayne Ltd during the 1960s.

Bypass Opens at Last

On 5th October 1970, the long-awaited Stromeferry bypass road was formally opened in a ceremony at Attadale Bridge by Secretary of State for Scotland Gordon Campbell.

The chairman of the County Council Highways Committee, Sir John Hayes, gave special thanks to his predecessor John Macdonald of Applecross for his efforts in ensuring the road was built, persuading the Scottish Development Department to contribute 75% of the total cost of £725,000.

Later, Mr Campbell opened an extension to Duncraig Castle College.

Postscript: In November the County Surveyor denied reports of problems with landslips on the road - though some loose stones, he conceded, had fallen from overhanging rockfaces...

Sign of the Times

South West Ross Field Club were given a talk in February on the development and operation of a fish-farm.

Tom Patey of Ullapool, one of Scotland's best-known climbers, fell to his death while descending a stack off the north coast of Sutherland in May. He had been the GP in Ullapool since the early 1960s.

New Vessel for Kyle

A new boat, *Kyleakin*, began operating on the Kyle-Kyleakin ferry service. She carried up to 28 cars, four times as many as the boats currently in service, with cars boarding and disembarking on a drive-through basis, much quicker than the existing side-loading operation. A sister vessel, *Lochalsh*, arrived to start work in 1971; both remained on the route for 20 years. The five vessels previously on the service were transferred elsewhere.

New Ship for Plockton

The Dulverton Trust charity commissioned a new three-masted sailing ship from a boatyard at Buckie. The vessel, to be based in Plockton, would serve as a training ship for a 36-strong crew aged 16-21. The management committee, which included Plockton residents, gave the 320-ton schooner the name *Captain Scott*. An itinerary of nine cruises, each of 26 days duration, was drawn up.

1970 (continued)

The thrice-weekly Kyle-Glenelg ferry service was withdrawn.

The National Trust for Scotland bought Shieldaig Island from their Coastline and Islands Fund. The cost was re-imbursed in 1974 by an American couple who had informally 'adopted' the island.

Hamish Gray unexpectedly won Ross-shire for the Conservatives at the General Election, defeating Liberal MP Alasdair Mackenzie.

Ross and Cromarty County Council discussed at length the recently published Wheatley report, which assessed alternatives for the first major changes in local government since 1930. Under the reforms subsequently introduced, Lewis was separated from Ross-shire and community councils set up *(see 1975)*.

Self-Service

Family grocers W.Spark & Sons brought a new concept to Wester Ross when they opened a self-service *Centra* shop at their Lochcarron premises.

Lochbroom Amenities Association requested the resumption of film shows by the Highlands & Islands Film Guild.

Country Festival

Following her visit to Shieldaig in May, Princess Margaret travelled to Gairloch to open the Festival of the Countryside. Spread over a fortnight and featuring events throughout Wester and South-West Ross, the festival was promoted by the Wester Ross Tourist Organisation and Highlands & Islands Development Board as part of European Conservation Year. It was hailed a success and plans made to repeat it.

New Minister

In 1970, Jackie Ross arrived in Lochcarron as the new Free Presbyterian Church minister. Four years earlier, he and some friends had founded the Blythswood Tract Society in Glasgow, to produce and distribute Christian literature in several languages. In 1977 the Society's head office was moved from Glasgow to Lochcarron. By the end of the decade, several Christian bookshops, a book van service and a wholesale book department had been set up in the Highlands *(see 1987)*.

Challenging Times at School

New School Opens But Two Close

Loch Duich Primary School in Inverinate opened in November. But this was not entirely good news for the area, because the school replaced not only the old school at Inverinate but those in two nearby townships, Shiel Bridge and Letterfearn.

Earlier that year, at a public meeting in Letterfearn, the community had expressed concern that their school was earmarked for closure by Ross & Cromarty County Council. They had recently seen their post office and shop close, one of the two mobile shops had ceased operating, and local people were anxious not to lose any more services - especially the school.

But protests were to no avail. From November, local children had to travel by bus to and from Inverinate. Mrs Gillies of Shiel School became the new Head Teacher at Loch Duich Primary, with Mrs Fraser of the old Inverinate School as her assistant. Mrs MacLean of Letterfearn School was transferred to Dornie School as Head Teacher, her assistant being Mrs MacLean, who was already there.

Craig School Closes

Due to the departure from the district of several families, the number of pupils at Craig School near Achnashellach had lately fallen to three. It was decided to close the school and transfer the pupils, along with the teacher Miss Stewart, to Lochcarron Primary School.

On the school's final day, a large company assembled for the annual prize-giving, with the three remaining pupils, Edith Robertson, Caroline MacLennan and Anne Mackay, receiving awards from Miss Milner, the former visiting music teacher. Miss Stewart reminisced about her twelve years in charge of the school, and thanked pupils and parents, past and present. The children entertained the gathering with a musical pogramme.

Laide School also closed in 1970.

Call for Better Facilities

The headmaster of Plockton High School, Sorley MacLean, commented on the school's shortage of facilities at the annual prize-giving. The building had been designed for 115 pupils in the mid-1960s but, since then, children from Lochcarron, Applecross and Shieldaig had been transferred from Dingwall Academy. There were now 202 pupils, having to share, by way of example, a single science room, one technical room and one handicraft room *(see 1975)*.

Gairloch Community Association called for Dingwall Academy to put back its opening time on Monday mornings to 10am, to allow west coast children to return from a weekend at home "without having to get out of bed at an unearthly hour."

The Wester Ross Provincial Mod was cancelled due to the lack of music teachers in the area.

BUTEC Base for Kyle

The early 1970s brought a significant employment boost for South-West Ross with the decision by the Ministry of Defence to establish the British Underwater Testing and Evaluation Centre (BUTEC) in the Inner Sound.

In 1970 surveys of possible sites for a missile range were carried out. The Scottish Office gave clearance in 1971 and the BUTEC 'concept document' was finalised in 1972. Kyle was to be the shore base, with a Range Terminal Building (RTB) set up at Applecross.

British Rail initially offered land for a base around Kyle railway station, as at that time the line was scheduled to close. In fact, it survived and the land for the base was subsequently reclaimed from the sea. The location of the RTB at Sand, Applecross, was the catalyst for the completion of the north Applecross coast road, with the MoD providing funding. BUTEC became the main employer in Wester Ross.

Toscaig Ferry Reprieved

A decision by the Scottish Transport Group (STG) to withdraw the Kyle-Toscaig ferry caused concern in Applecross, and was referred to a hearing in Kyle of the Scottish Transport Users' Consultative Committee for Scotland, who subsequently objected.

At the hearing, the STG reported that the ferry had made a loss of £4,000 in 1969. The company were not prepared to run it unless the County Council made good the deficit. The Council, Lochcarron District Council and the Applecross Committee urged that the service be continued until a road was built round the north coast of Applecross; if it was withdrawn before then, there might be no community left for the road to serve. In April 1971 the ferry's future was safeguarded when the Scottish Office agreed to pay 75% of annual operating costs or £5000 (whichever less). The ferry operated until the road was completed in 1976.

Kyle Loses the Stornoway Ferry

In January 1970, Willie Ross, Secretary of State for Scotland, awaited detailed recommendations from the Scottish Transport Group, which included David MacBrayne Ltd, on the future of the Western Isles ferry service, and the case for an Ullapool-Stornoway service.

The Scottish Transport Group duly announced that an Ullapool-Stornoway service would be included in their future developments. The STG commissioned designs and costings for new piers at Ullapool and Stornoway.

The Group's Chairman subsequently announced that, if the service's mainland base was to be Ullapool, almost certainly the Kyle-Stornoway ferry service would have to cease. However, Kyle would still have an important role to play as the main gateway to Skye.

People in Lochalsh, however, were understandably upset. Torquil Nicolson, Plockton, chairman of South-West Ross District Council, pointed out that not only were fourteen local jobs at risk, but possibly the future of the railway between Inverness and Kyle.

Meanwhile Ross and Cromarty County Council had already set up a 'Stornoway/ Mainland Ferry Service' sub-committee to examine the matter. The County Council and local harbour commissions arranged a meeting for February. A request that Aultbea should be considered as a possible ferry port was taken into account too.

In October, the County Council voted on which port or ports should in future provide a mainland link with Stornoway. Voting went in favour of Ullapool by 31 to 8; the proposal for Aultbea was defeated by the same margin, 8 to 31.

A proposal to retain a service at Kyle was also defeated, by the smaller margin of 22 to 16, which meant that several councillors evidently believed it would be viable to operate a service from both Kyle and Ullapool. It was not to be. Ullapool replaced Kyle as the port for Stornoway in 1973.

Unique Postal Service

The Summer Isles Postal service was inaugurated on Tanera Mor. Using specially printed postage stamps, it remains one of only two private postal services in Britain. A first-day cover was presented to the Queen during her annual voyage round the north-west coast in *Britannia* prior to the Royal Family's stay at Balmoral.

Tourism & Beauty News

At the start of the year, Wester Ross Tourist Organisation took over responsibility for marketing the area from more local tourist associations such as Gairloch & Wester Ross Tourist Association and Lochbroom Tourist Association. Each local association elected members onto a new committee.

In January the new Tourist Organisation staged a *Miss Wester Ross* contest. Eight girls - two each from Locharron, Gairloch, South West Ross and Lochbroom - competed, the contest being won by Esther Fraser from Inverinate, who went on to compete for the *Miss Highlands & Islands* title.

Beauty contests were in vogue at this time - and still politically correct. Members of Ross & Cromarty Liberal Association elected a *North-West Ross Princess.*

The Tourist Organisation reported a good year for enquiries at local information centres in 1969 - 25,000 at Kyle alone. They approached the County Council for funds to employ extra staff at Kyle and Gairloch, and built an area office at Gairloch. A new permanent information centre was also opened at Lochcarron Village Hall, making four manned offices in all (Kyle, Lochcarron, Gairloch and Ullapool). Unmanned information points were sited at Kinlochewe, Dornie and Glenshiel. And at a meeting in December, the Tourist Organisation outlined plans for the coming season including a new centre at Kyle.

Respect the Sabbath

Gairloch Community Association requested the Wester Ross Tourist Organisation not to open the local information centre on Sundays.

Proposals for the registration of tourism businesses, under the 1969 Tourism Act, were discussed. It was agreed to press the Scottish Tourist Board to give the Highlands a fair share of national advertising.

Aultguish Inn, managed for many years by Anne Bruce on behalf of the Lochluichart Estate, was sold.

A community meeting in Aultbea called for more public toilets to be provided in North-West Ross. The only loos were in Ullapool and Gairloch.

C.Pashley

Left: Ullapool & District Junior Pipe Band entertain the crowds at Lochcarron Highland Games

Below: Gairloch developed steadily during the century but retains its peaceful charm in a superb setting

Bottom: Wintry scene at Ullapool

C.Pashley

C.Pashley

Above: The Ninian Central Platform takes shape at the Kishorn Fabrication Yard in 1976-77. After initial construction at the shore base, it was towed out into the loch where work continued.

Below: The finished platform is towed through the Inner Sound, bound for the North Sea

C.Pashley

The Seventies

Achtercairn Junior Secondary School, Gairloch, was downgraded in status to a two-year secondary, which meant that pupils would have to transfer to Dingwall Academy from their third year onwards.

There was shock when British Rail announced that the railway to Kyle would close at the end of 1973. The Conservative government had refused to renew grant support for the line. The news sparked a long campaign of opposition, but it was not until mid-1974, with the prospect of the oil industry coming to Kishorn, that the new Labour government gave an assurance the line would remain open.

A causeway over Loch Duich, by-passing Morvich, was formally opened by the Secretary of State for Scotland. The causeway shortened the route of the A87 between the Great Glen and the west coast by two miles. At the opening ceremony, local councillor Torquil Nicolson regretted that travellers on their way to and from Stornoway would not have long to enjoy the benefits of the newly reconstructed A87, since Kyle was soon to be replaced as the ferry port for Stornoway by Ullapool.

The weekly left-wing newspaper the *West Highland Free Press* was launched, serving Skye, South-West Ross, the Outer Isles and, to a lesser extent, Wester Ross.

Wester Ross was in the national headlines as the Drumbuie inquiry got under way at Balmacara *(see below)*.

Drumbuie, Kishorn and the Oil Platform Industry

A proposal to establish an oil drilling platform fabrication yard at Drumbuie in Lochalsh in 1973 was met with a strong campaign of opposition. Many felt the long-term risks to the local community outweighed the possible short-term benefits. A lengthy public inquiry was held at Balmacara, resulting in the proposal being rejected.

This was the era of the first North Sea oil boom. Competition to construct drilling platforms was increasing, and attention had turned to possible construction sites on the west coast. The Taylor Woodrow Mowlem consortium applied to build platforms at either of two locations in Wester Ross: Ullapool or Drumbuie. Local action groups were formed in both places to oppose development. In the autumn the Ullapool option was eliminated.

The Scottish Office referred the application for Drumbuie to a public inquiry which opened at Balmacara in November. The plan had the support of the Highlands & Islands Development Board. The opposition case was presented partly by the National Trust for Scotland as landowners, but also by the County Council and local groups. One of their main contentions was that the development would not create long-term local employment as promised.

The consortium's case centred on the need for a deep-water site to undertake construction of the 'Condeep' design of platform for which their current site at Alness was unsuitable.

At the end of 1973 the Conservative Government indicated they might intervene with a compulsory purchase order, to resolve the inquiry. However, the Tories' defeat at the general election in February 1974 ended fears of this happening. In June, the Inquiry Reporter commented that the project would be a gross intrusion on the landscape and would introduce a caste system common in industrial areas but inappropriate in a crofting community. In August the Secretary of State rejected the application.

Kishorn

In December 1973, while the Drumbuie inquiry proceeded, Sir John Howard & Co, together with the French engineering company C.G.Doris, lodged an application to build oil drilling platforms on the north shore of Loch Kishorn. This proposal won the qualified support of the local community.

No public inquiry was held into the Kishorn scheme, partly because there was less opposition but also because the Drumbuie inquiry had already provided so much relevant evidence. Planning permission for the Howard Doris site was given in September 1974.

The development was to provide a unique boost to employment and prosperity in the area for the next decade. At the same time, it effectively safeguarded the future of the Kyle railway, which had been under threat of closure since 1971, by virtue of an agreement that most supplies and equipment for the fabrication yard would be delivered by rail to sidings at Stromeferry, then shipped across Loch Carron. This arrangement, with the yard designated an 'island site', lasted until 1982. However, inevitably, there was also a large amount of road traffic along the single-track route between Lochcarron and Kishorn, operated in convoys accompanied by escort vehicles.

A dry dock was created in 1974 and in 1975 production work on the huge *Ninian Central Platform* began. Built of concrete and weighing 600,000 tons, it was the biggest floating structure ever constructed. (The sister platform *Ninian Northern* was built at Nigg by Highland Fabricators.) *Ninian Central* was towed out into the loch in 1976, and work completed by 1977.

At busy times, the yard was open all hours. In late 1975 the Chairman of Howard Doris, Sir John Howard, together with Managing Director Albert Granville, had urged the local community to allow work on Sundays and at a public meeting in Lochcarron a secret ballot consented by a majority of six, 87 to 81.

Workers at the Kishorn yard were recruited both locally and outside the area, with accommodation for incomers provided in a local camp and in new houses at Lochcarron. Company executives stayed at Achnashellach Lodge.

The development of the yard was good news for the community not only in providing employment for those already there, but also by attracting back to the area many who had moved away.

One of the first steps taken on behalf of the local community when the yard opened was to secure the formation of the Howard Doris Trust, funded by contributions from the consortium. Its aim was to assist community projects and young people's training, and this was achieved before the fund was wound up in the late 1990s.

Production work at Kishorn continued for 12 years. The site's other great construction achievement, apart from the *Ninian Central*, was the *Maureen* hi-deck steel platform *(see 1980)*.

In March, Ullapool replaced Kyle as the mainland port for MacBrayne's ferry service to Stornoway. It was the first time for many years, since the days of *Clansman* and *Claymore*, that Ullapool had enjoyed a ferry connection to Lewis.

Caledonian MacBrayne was formed when the Scottish Transport Group merged the MacBrayne's operation with Clyde-based Caledonian Steam Packet Co.

Balmacara House School was closed by the County Council. A survey of past students indicated that few of the boys being trained in agriculture were actually going into farming. The building was found a new use in 1978 when it was leased to the Ministry of Defence to accommodate BUTEC staff.

The Royal Mail introduced its first postbus services in Wester Ross, between Kinlochewe and Alligin, and Kyle and Letterfearn. This was not, however, a new idea in the area, where local operators had always carried both passengers and mail.

Sabhal Mor Ostaig, a Gaelic education college, was established on Skye.

The *Ullapool News*, a weekly paper, was launched. The 60-bedroom Mercury Motor Inn was opened in Ullapool.

1974

Highland Fish Farmers Ltd started in business near Strome, Loch Carron. The firm has steadily grown and is now a major employer in the district.

The new oilrig platform construction yard at Kishorn started work on its first order *(see previous page)*.

A new two-tier structure was created for local government in the Highlands, with Highland Regional Council taking over many functions from Ross and Cromarty County Council. Meanwhile Ross & Cromarty District Council was set up with responsibility for housing and other services as far south-west as Strathcarron. South-West Ross was now covered by Skye & Lochalsh District Council. Four former District Councils in Wester Ross were dissolved, to be replaced over the next two years by smaller Community Councils.

Policing was also re-organised in 1975, with Ross and Sutherland Constabulary absorbed into Northern Constabulary.

Plockton's former school, closed since the mid-1960s when the new High School was built, re-opened as Plockton Primary School. With pupil numbers increasing (a trend not foreseen in the 1960s) the High School building had proved too small to accommodate both secondary and primary children.

At one of their last meetings, the County Council discussed a plan to convert the former Morefield Hotel, Ullapool, which they had purchased, into an old people's home. In the event, to the indignation of many, the building was demolished.

1976

The final section of the North Applecross coast road between Cuaig and Applecross was opened, with much of the funding provided by the MoD who required access to their new Range Terminal Building at Sand. The MoD subsequently purchased 5.5 acres of coastline from the Applecross Estate.

Wester Ross Tourist Organisation opened a new information centre at Achtercairn.

1977

Highland Regional Council opened a new pier at Gairloch Harbour. The local community had been pressing for this for some years.

Gairloch Heritage Museum was opened at Achtercairn.

The Automobile Association unveiled its highest viewpoint near the 2052 feet summit of the Bealach na Ba.

Gairloch and District Sheepdog Trials were revived after 13 years.

A landfill site was opened on former common grazings at Morefield, Ullapool.

Ullapool & District Junior Pipe Band was established. The first public performance was given two years later, since when the band has given great pleasure with regular appearances throughout the north each year.

1978

Wester Ross Salmon, a fish-farming business, was established near Ullapool.

The *Gairloch & District Times* was launched as a fortnightly community newspaper.

Achtercairn School, Gairloch, was upgraded from two-year to four-year status.

Under a new arrangement, children from Lochinver were allowed to attend Ullapool School, travelling south every day instead of staying in hostel accommodation at Golspie in East Sutherland during the week. This arrangement was later made permanent.

Isle Martin was given by Mrs Goldsmith as a Nature Reserve to the Royal Society for the Protection of Birds.

In December the Marquesa de Torrehermosa, proprietor of Strathbran estate, entertained staff and their friends to a Christmas party.

Return of the Klondykers

Fishing for herring was banned for three years in 1977 to conserve stocks. The herring fishery had by this time, in any event, been declining for several years. But as though to compensate, there was the beginning of a long upsurge in mackerel fishing at Ullapool. Foreign factory ships, which soon became known as klondykers, a term not heard locally since the First World War, arrived in Loch Broom to trans-ship and process fish caught by Scottish boats. Scottish mackerel catches doubled between 1976 and 1977, and for the first time most of the catch was for human consumption.

Above: The Hydroponicum, Achiltibuie, seen in 1986

Right: The Dornie bridge, with the old ferry slipway in the foreground

Bottom: One of the foreign 'Klondyker' factory ships which made Ullapool and Loch Broom a busy place in the 1980s. This is Russian ship Kaliningradski Bereg

The Eighties and Nineties

During the last 20 years of the century the slight increase of population noted in the 1970s was maintained - which was progress in itself. Many incomers from elsewhere in Scotland and south of the border were attracted to the area by the quality of life, especially with the improvement in services in recent times.

Education facilities improved: a new wing was built at Plockton High School in 1980 and new High Schools at Gairloch and Ullapool in the 1990s. Other new community facilities included health centres, leisure centres, swimming pools, libraries and museums. Many projects were achieved after local campaigns.

Further road improvements were made in the 1980s, notably the doubling of 15 miles of the A832 between Gorstan and Achnasheen. Unfortunately the 1990s saw a slowdown in investment.

In the 1990s, rapid progress in telecommunications and computer technology enabled a number of businesses to be set up and run locally without the limitations previously imposed by geographical remoteness.

Growing interest in Gaelic was reflected in the establishment of Gaelic-medium education units at four local primary schools.

Not all was rosy by any means. As incomers arrived, so house prices went up, making it difficult for young local people to buy property - and many did continue to move away. The Kishorn platform fabrication yard closed in the late 1980s. The Klondykers brought welcome business to Ullapool - but moved away from Loch Broom in the mid-1990s.

As fish-farming continued to expand, numbers of wild salmon fell. Fuel costs rose, which greatly affects the cost of living in this area. Visitor numbers peaked in 1990 and have since been affected by factors including the high cost of petrol, cheap foreign travel, a strong pound, and keen competition from other areas.

Diary of a Year

1980

School to Close?

The future of Achmore School, whose survival had been in doubt for several years, was discussed again by the Regional Council. The current school roll of five, which was the minimum necessary to keep a school open, was expected to fall to three in May. Local residents complained that new housing, long promised, had not been built, and this limited the number of children who could live in the community. Sadly, Achmore School closed in 1981.

A new wing was opened in Plockton High School.

Ullapool School Upgraded

There was satisfaction when Ullapool School was upgraded to four-year secondary status. Due to a shortage of houses for new teaching staff, the District Council allocated the next three council house vacancies to married teachers - a useful gesture, as 64 families were currently on the Council waiting-list.

At a meeting in Gairloch, parents called for the further upgrading of Achtercairn School to full six-year status.

School Accolade

Pupils of Achnasheen Primary School were given a trip to Nova Scotia as guests of the people of Truro in recognition of their work creating a folk museum at the school. Additional funding for their expenses was offered by the Howard Doris Trust and Strathgarve & Contin Community Council.

New Clan Chief

At a ceremony in Inverness, Ronnie MacLennan, a Physical Education teacher in Ullapool, was formally recognised as the 34th Chief of Clan MacLennan - the first for several centuries. The Clan MacLennan Association had recently opened a museum and visitor centre at the head of Loch Duich in Kintail, their original home territory.

Pool Wanted

Ullapool residents campaigned for a swimming-pool. A pool was currently included in Ross & Cromarty District Council's five-year plan, but the Council had advised that, due to cutbacks, it would not be feasible to build it for some time.

Highland Health Board gave details of new surgeries at Aultbea and Ullapool.

More Good News at Kishorn

Albert Granville, Managing Director of Howard Doris Ltd, Kishorn, spoke to the company's staff at a New Year dinner-dance in Stromeferry Hotel, expressing optimism for the future of the yard. A major contract was in hand to build the steel integrated deck of the Maureen platform for Phillips Petroleum. New cranes, a 1000-ton crane barge and a jack-up rig were to be delivered on-site soon. He called on Highland Regional Council to improve the Kishorn-Lochcarron road, and on British Rail to give assurances about the future of the Kyle railway. In February, Kishorn's new jack-up rig was christened the *Casan Mor* by the wife of the Project Manager for Phillips's Maureen Field.

Howard Doris announced in March that they had also won a contract to build the Maureen's single-point mooring loading platform, and to design and build the concrete section of the structure, which would serve as a platform for the loading of tankers. This structure, 430 feet high, was built in the dry dock. There were 600 workers at Kishorn in November 1980, and the firm stated this should increase to 1,600 in 1981. Meanwhile Highland Fabricators in Easter Ross were also busy, expanding their Nigg site by 100 acres.

In 1983 Prince Charles performed the dedication ceremony for the completed *Maureen* platform.

Tourism News

A proposal to amalgamate the Wester Ross and Easter Ross Tourist Organisations prompted protests from west-coast members. But the two bodies were eventually merged in 1983 to form the Ross & Cromarty Tourist Board.

Wester Ross Hoteliers Association ran a spring break package called *Coastaround*, which was a success and repeated in following years. A new walks leaflet was published by the Wester Ross Tourist Organisation.

After a disappointing season, the Easter Ross Tourist Organisation closed their Tourist Office at Tarvie a month earlier than planned.

The Highlands and Islands Tourism Council sent a mailshot to 20,000 homes throughout the UK. Meanwhile the HIDB and Scottish Tourist Board jointly launched a pilot scheme to classify accommodation according to bedroom facilities, public rooms, services and meals.

Industrial Estate to Open

The Scottish Development Authority funded the construction of a light industrial estate at Achiltibuie.

1980 (continued)

A football pitch was laid out at Morefield, and a path built to link the new local housing estate to Ullapool.

Gairloch Community Council voiced concern about the numbers of livestock roaming round the village, despite new cattle-grids and fencing.

Plans were made to improve the Battery Park in Lochcarron.

It was announced that Kyle Telephone Exchange would close in 1984.

The Tenants' Rights (Scotland) Bill proposed the sale of council houses.

Friendly Rivalry

The Gairloch & District Times rather grudgingly admitted that the local football team had lost a recent match. *The winning goal came from Taylor, the Ullapool winger, who hit the ball with his thigh, knee and shin before it hit the post and rolled over the line.*

Aultbea Community Council called for a Second World War gun-pit at Aird to be preserved as a memorial. Gun housings at Cove were also still in place; and in the late 1990s a memorial to the men who sailed with the Arctic convoys was erected nearby.

A transmitter mast was built at Braes above Ullapool.

Museum Accolade

Gairloch and District Heritage Society was formed by the local members' group of Ross and Cromarty Heritage Society. The group already managed the local museum, which was awarded the title of *Scottish Museum of the Year* in July. Meanwhile the museum acquired the hull of one of the last surviving local 'Zulu' fishing-boats, *Queen Mary*. Built at Alligin in 1911, this boat was currently rotting on the shoreline at Badachro. Kenny Mackenzie, one of her former crew, still lived locally at Aird Farm, Aultbea. Gairloch Heritage Museum later acquired another boat, *Ribhinn Bhoidheach*, built in 1914 at Port Henderson.

Trouble at Sea

Dispute over Trawling

Creel fishermen from Torridon, Gairloch and Aultbea passed a motion urging that only passive fishing methods be permitted within three miles of the shore - in other words, a ban on trawling, which it was feared was damaging the sea-bed. The move came at a meeting of Gairloch branch of the West Coast Static Gear Fishermen's Association in March. The meeting also called for more regional management of fisheries, the current system of central government control being out of touch.

In August, creel fishermen based at Gairloch voiced concern that, following the start of the mackerel fishing season, they had had to withdraw from certain fishing grounds to avoid the risk of east-coast trawlers damaging their gear. And in a fresh outbreak of tension in September, creelmen prevented hauliers from unloading fish from trawlers at Gairloch pier, by blockading the access road with their cars.

Disputes between creel fishermen and trawlermen continued to simmer during the 1980s until in 1991 all trawling in Loch Gairloch was banned and other sea-lochs further south were closed between October and March each year.

More Disputes and Developments

After French fishing firm Jego Quere sought permission to build a £1.5m fish-processing plant at Kyle, local fishermen organised a blockade, preventing French trawlers from landing at the harbour. The local men feared the plan would lead to a decline in the local industry and to over-fishing.

Marine Harvest Ltd were given permission by the Crown Estate to establish salmon-farming operations in Loch Duich, Loch Ewe and Loch Torridon.

Not in My Back Yard

When a planning application to establish a fish-farm at Tanera Mor was discussed by Coigach Community Council, one member wondered whether a more suitable site might not be found for it.

'Norway', suggested another.

Pier Dues Controversy

Ullapool Pier Trustees applied for a Provisional Order to increase their jurisdiction over an area including the whole of the sea east of a line betweeen Greenstone Point and Reiff, taking in Gruinard Bay and Little Loch Broom.

The move followed the rapid expansion of the mackerel fishery at Ullapool in the previous three years. Growing numbers of factory ships were now mooring over a wide area of Loch Broom and Annat Bay for weeks or months at a time.

But Coigach Community Council strongly opposed the plan as the enlarged area took in the pier at Badentarbet. The Trustees subsequently reduced their designated area.

Meanwhile, to meet demand for accommodation by fish buyers a number of portakabins were erected at Ullapool harbour, which remained in place until the end of the klondyking era in the mid-1990s.

Ullapool staged the British Skate-Fishing Championship in July as part of its sea-angling festival week.

A salmon smokehouse was established at Altandubh.

Highland Regional Council discussed how to deal with the large numbers of people staying in caravans in Ullapool due to a shortage of permanent accommodation.

Gaelic was restored as a subject on the curriculum at Plockton Primary School, with tuition given by a visiting teacher.

Work began on a sheltered housing complex in Ullapool, to be called Lochbroom House & Fraser Court.

Edmund Mackenzie opened a craft shop on Harbour Street, Plockton, later to be famous in the TV series *Hamish Macbeth.*

Strathpeffer Station was restored and converted to a craft centre incorporating the Highland Museum of Childhood.

A Scottish Office report identified five suitable sites for superquarries in Scotland, including one by Loch Ewe.

Lochcarron Community Council called for a water supply to be provided at Strathcarron.

Ross and Cromarty District Council called for a revival of the project for a hydro-electric scheme at Fionn Loch.

Old Days on the Roads

Hector Macleod, Gairloch, retired after 45 years as a Roads Supervisor with the County (latterly Regional) Council. At a presentation in the Old Inn, he recalled how, in the mid-1930s, the only tarmac surfaces in the whole of Wester Ross were on one or two streets in Ullapool. Other roads were gravel or metal. "In snowy weather, a type of sledge weighed down with sandbags towed by a lorry was the only snow-plough. If a sandbag fell off, then one of the roadmen had to take its place!"

*In the table opposite, places listed are 'settlement zones': Lochcarron, for example, includes Strathcarron. The source is Highland Regional Council (figures based on the census). Note that one likely factor behind the decrease of population at Lochcarron and nearby communities was the closure of Kishorn oil platform construction yard in the late 1980s.

A Growing Population

In the 1980s the population increase noted in the 1970s was consolidated in most districts of Wester Ross.

District*	1981	1991	% change
Achiltibuie	259	290	Up 12%
Ullapool	1350	1558	Up 15%
Dundonnell	163	169	Up 4%
Scoraig	84	88	Up 5%
Lochbroom parish	*1856*	*2105*	*Up 13%*
Aultbea	536	596	Up 11%
Poolewe	206	218	Up 6%
Inverasdale	149	198	Up 33%
Gairloch	955	1061	Up 11%
Kinlochewe	88	107	Up 22%
Gairloch parish	*1934*	*2180*	*Up 13%*
Torridon	214	198	Down 7%
Shieldaig	167	146	Down 13%
Applecross	233	222	Down 5%
Applecross parish	*614*	*566*	*Down 9%*
Lochcarron	930	871	Down 6%
Achmore	83	120	Up 45%
Plockton	425	452	Up 6%
Kyle	874	871	-
Balmacara	267	270	Up 1%
Lochalsh parish	*1649*	*1713*	*Up 1%*
Dornie	266	266	-
Inverinate	362	404	Up 12%
Killilan	119	123	Up 3%
Kintail/Glenshiel	*747*	*793*	*Up 6%*
Total (7 parishes)	7730	8228	Up 6%
Other areas			
Achnasheen	47	44	Down 6%
Garve	279	304	Up 9%
Glenelg	267	229	Down 14%

Gairloch Heritage Museum showing the two locally built boats, and the light from Rubha Reidh Lighthouse

Eighties and Nineties

1981

A transmitter was erected at Duncraig, enabling viewers in Plockton to receive colour television pictures for the first time.

Killilan School closed.

The Kessock Bridge was opened by the Queen Mother in August. With a new approach road across the Black Isle from Maryburgh via Tore, the journey time between Wester Ross and Inverness was now greatly reduced. The Kessock ferry ceased operating. The construction of a new direct road betweeen Contin and Maryburgh several years later reduced journey times even more.

There was shock throughout Ross-shire when the British Aluminium Company abruptly closed its Invergordon smelter in February, just 11 years after it was opened. 900 jobs were lost.

1983

It was announced that Achtercairn School, Gairloch, and Ullapool School, were to be upgraded from four-year to six-year secondary status. The cost of necessary improvements to the school buildings was estimated at £275,000. However, this would be offset by savings of £100,000 per annum from the closure of the two hostels at Dingwall Academy which accommodated west-coast boys and girls. When sixth-year pupils came through at Achtercairn in 1985, the school was re-named Gairloch High School.

Gaelic-medium primary school units opened at Portree and Inverness.

Tourist Boards for South West Ross & Skye, and Ross & Cromarty, were established. The merger of the Wester Ross and Easter Ross Tourist Organisations was controversial, many members of the WRTO objecting.

Ullapool's new health centre opened.

Lochcarron Shinty Club, celebrating their centenary, won the Strathdearn Cup.

Ill Fares the Land, a film about the evacuation of St Kilda, was shot in Lochalsh and Applecross.

During severe storms, hundreds of trees were blown down at Inverewe and Attadale Gardens. Cables in the Kishorn district were also brought down, causing a freak electrical fault which resulted in cookers and fridges glowing red-hot, and one cottage burned down.

1985

The monthly community magazine *An Carrannach* was launched, serving the area between Strathcarron and Torridon.

Rubha Reidh lighthouse near Melvaig was converted to automatic operation.

Scenes for the film *Highlander*, starring Sean Connery, were shot at Eilean Donan Castle. The film's premiere was held at Inverness in 1986. The castle featured in a James Bond movie in the 1990s.

The First Challenge

The Great Wilderness Challenge was staged for the first time, attracting 178 runners and walkers. The aim of this remarkable event was to raise money from sponsorship for charity, and the first year's total of £6,200 was given to the Highland Hospice; in later years a range of charities, including the Hospice, was supported. Three events were staged, over 25 miles, 13 miles and 7 miles, each taking in some of the finest scenery in Britain between Little Loch Broom and Loch Ewe *(see 2000)*.

Kinloch Damph Ltd, nowadays a major employer in Wester Ross, started business as salmon smolt producers.

BUTEC, the British Underwater Testing and Evaluation Centre, took over the boatyard of Maclean & Macrae, Kyle.

Major pier improvements were carried out at Ullapool harbour, including the construction of an ice-making plant.

The Hydroponicum, Achiltibuie, which is now one of the most popular attractions in Wester Ross, was opened by Robert Irvine of the Summer Isles Hotel. Its claim to fame is its unusual method of cultivating vegetables and fruit using nutrients and water but no soil.

End of an Era
Kishorn Yard Closes

In the absence of new orders, Howard Doris Ltd went into receivership and their oil platform fabrication yard at Kishorn closed. Several attempts have been made since then to re-open the site, most

Blythswood in Romania

On behalf of the Lochcarron-based charity the Blythswood Tract Society, Reverend Jackie Ross *(see 1970)* and his brother Don embarked on a pioneering aid mission to Romania in 1987. Having crammed a van full of food, medicines, clothing and books, they were overwhelmed by the gratitude they were shown when they distributed the goods in the town of Oradea.

It was to be the first of many such missions to eastern Europe. In 1988 Jackie, with his wife and family, made another trip, developing contacts and learning about the Romanians' needs. For the Romanians, in the days of Ceausescu and the notorious State Police the *Securitate*, it was risky even to speak to Jackie.

Back home, Blythswood set themselves a target of raising £80,000 to fund further aid missions. Some of the money was diverted to victims of the Armenian earthquake.

In 1990 the Romanian revolution eased the challenge of getting supplies into the country, and regular missions were sent out. Hospitals and orphanages were among the main beneficiaries.

New depots were opened in the Highlands, an appeals co-ordinator was appointed, and missions were also sent to Albania and Yugoslavia. In 1992 Rona Mackenzie of Lochcarron was sent out to Romania as a resident helper.

In the years that have followed, Blythswood International have been synonymous with aid work throughout Eastern Europe. A network of charity shops and storage depots and the goodwill of countless supporters have helped maintain the effort. Jackie Ross died in 2002 but his work goes on.

coming to nothing. In 1991, a contract was lost to a rival bidder, MacDermott's of Ardersier. Caissons for the Skye Bridge were built at the yard. In 1994 the Costain Taylor Woodrow consortium considered using the site. In 2000, Kishorn Base Ltd was formed to try to attract rig-decommissioning work.

A new community swimming-pool at Poolewe opened after several years of fund-raising and campaigning.

Ullapool celebrated its bicentenary. The disused Parliamentary Church on West Argyle Street was used as the venue for an exhibition which attracted thousands of visitors. The church has since been restored as the permanent home of Ullapool Museum and Visitor Centre.

A secondary school opened at Scoraig. It closed again in 1994 when pupil numbers fell to one, but re-opened later.

The School Boards (Scotland) Act re-introduced local school boards.

Blaming rising costs and falling student applications, Highland Regional Council decided to close Duncraig Castle College.

A Gaelic-medium unit opened at Plockton Primary School.

Mail was delivered to Wester Ross by train for the last time.

A new pier extension was opened at Gairloch Harbour by Highland Regional Council at a cost of £1 million. The harbour recorded landings of 644 tons in 1990, mostly prawns, worth £1.13m. Local vessel *Prosperity* was the top prawn boat in the north-west.

The Scottish Transport Group was privatised but Caledonian MacBrayne remained a public body under the control of the Secretary of State for Scotland.

The Ministry of Defence reduced the workload at the BUTEC range at Kyle.

The newly formed Gaelic Broacasting Committee was awarded £8 million to invest in programmes during its first year.

A campaign for a swimming-pool at Kyle raised £36,000 among the local community. Donations from the Howard Doris Trust and SERCO (agents for the BUTEC range) helped realise the target of £100,000. Skye & Lochalsh District Council agreed to meet running costs.

In April, Gruinard Island was declared free of anthrax contamination.

The death of Duncan Mackay, who had lived his whole life in a black house at Lonbain in Applecross, was reported.

Auchtertyre School was opened, replacing Lochalsh school in the same township. Dornie School was closed, its pupils transferring to Auchtertyre.

A Trust in Lochcarron made plans to establish a museum at the old smithy.

Shinty was re-introduced to the sports curriculum at Plockton High School. Shinty flourished in Wester Ross during the 1990s, partly inspired by Skye's victory in the Camanachd Cup final of 1990.

Intermediate stations on the Kyle line became unstaffed.

1991

Skye Bridge Designed

A design for the proposed bridge to Skye was chosen by the Scottish Office. Modifications were later made in response to objections from, among others, the National Trust for Scotland as proprietors of Lochalsh Estate, who argued that it should be more sympathetic to its unique environment. Some parties, meantime, still argued for a tunnel rather than a bridge, others for a 24-hour ferry. Even more contentious in coming years would be the cost of the bridge and who was going to meet it - the taxpayer or tollpayers. In due course the construction contract was controversially awarded to a private consortium who were given the right to levy tolls in return.

Too Late...

Caledonian MacBrayne announced the introduction of a 24-hour service on the Kyle-Kyleakin ferry from April.

A new Dornie bridge was opened.

Loch Gairloch was permanently closed to trawlers under powers of the Inshore Fishing (Scotland) Act of 1984. The aim was to protect the sea-bed from being damaged. Trawling in sea-lochs between Loch Torridon and Loch Hourn was prohibited between October and March.

Amazon Seafoods Ltd, which had started at Kyleakin in the 1970s before moving to Kyle, opened a factory at Gairloch *(see 1998)*.

Salmon Leaps Ahead

Scottish salmon-farms harvested 40,600 tons of fish in 1991. In the same year, catches of wild salmon amounted to barely one per cent of that total (463 tons), using the three traditional methods of rod and line (228 tons), bag-net and stake-net (137 tons), and net and boat (97 tons). By 1999, production of Scottish farmed salmon rose to 112,000 tons, with France alone buying 30,000 tons. The biggest producer in the world was Norway with 395,000 tons.

Scottish Natural Heritage (SNH) was formed by the merging of the Nature Conservancy Council for Scotland and the Countryside Commission for Scotland. Forest Enterprise became the commercial agency of the Forestry Commission.

The Ferguson Medical Centre was opened in Lochcarron.

A Gaelic Medium Unit was opened at Lochcarron Primary School.

A nursing home for the elderly, Mo Dhachaidh, was opened in Ullapool.

Forestry jobs were cut in Lochalsh.

Campaigners against the Skye Bridge reluctantly accepted that its construction was now inevitable and switched the focus of their protests to the collection of tolls.

Assynt Crofters Trust completed their historic purchase of North Assynt Estate.

The *Braer* tanker oil-spill off Shetland caused concerns about the risk of similar incidents occurring off the west coast.

Ullapool Primary School's new Gaelic Medium Unit was opened.

The Stromeferry Hotel was badly damaged in a fire.

High School Opens

The new Gairloch High School was formally opened in September. Headmaster Neil Wilkie paid tribute to those who had campaigned for it for many years, including George Ginn, former teacher and Councillor. Among its facilities the school included a community library and theatre. 201 pupils currently attended the High School, taught by 30 teachers.

Ullapool Swimming Pool was opened.

New health centres were opened in Gairloch and Torridon.

A Pictish stone believed to be 1500 years old was found in Poolewe churchyard.

Storm damage to sand dunes at Gairloch was repaired with 10,000 tons of sand and marram grass from Big Sand.

Achnasheen Hotel burned down.

Ross County were admitted to the Scottish Football League.

The Queen's Own Highlanders (Seaforths & Camerons) merged with the Gordon Highlanders to form the Highlanders.

1995

A lifeboat was stationed at Kyle by the RNLI. An impressive new lifeboat station was later built to house it.

Township's Accolade

In 1996 Drumbuie was declared *Crofting Township of the Year* by Scottish Natural Heritage and the Scottish Crofters Union. SCU president Alistair MacIver said Drumbuie 'highlighted what can be achieved on small crofts when everyone cooperates'.

The 17 crofts of the township were, unusually, all occupied and actively crofted, with 33 hectares of arable ground used to grow turnips, corn, potatoes, rape and winter hay. Local drainage had recently been renewed.

The land in and around Drumbuie is owned by the National Trust for Scotland, whose ranger organised township walks during the summer, taking in birds, marine life and wild flowers growing beside coastal fields.

Skye Bridge Opens

The Skye Bridge was formally opened on 16th October. The first tolls were collected, and the first of many protests were made by campaigners who refused to pay them. Several court cases in subsequent years examined the case that tolls were illegal, and though the argument was rejected, most would agree that the moral right was on the protesters' side.

The Venture Trust charitable organisation leased Hartfield House in Applecross to run rehabilitation courses for young offenders aged 16-25 *(see 2000)*.

A new vessel, *Isle of Lewis*, was built for the Ullapool-Stornoway ferry service.

Ullapool Museum opened.

The local community radio station Lochbroom FM was launched.

Existing area tourist boards serving South West Ross & Skye, and Ross & Cromarty, were controversially replaced by the Highlands of Scotland Tourist Board. Many locals opposed the decision.

A coastal protection scheme costing £350,000 was built at Shieldaig.

Torridon's new village hall was opened.

The lighthouse on Eilean Ban was decommissioned, with new lights attached to the Skye Bridge directly overhead.

Controversial Scheme

A public inquiry at Gairloch examined the case for a hydro-electric development at Shieldaig Forest. The 2.1 mw scheme involved damming Loch a' Bhelaich, Loch a' Ghobhainn and Loch Gainneamh and was promoted by Highland Light & Power Ltd with the co-operation of the Gairloch Estate. Planning consent was refused.

The A890 between Achasheen and Glencarron was re-built by Highland Council, the new six-mile road being opened in December. Widening the A832 from Achnasheen to Kinlochewe over Glen Docherty now became the council's top roads priority in Wester Ross.

Amazon Seafoods Ltd laid off staff at their processing factory at Gairloch harbour. At one time 45 workers had been employed. Amazon's Kyle factory continued in business.

Inverasdale School was reprieved after a campaign of opposition to its closure.

Ullapool Golf Course was opened.

Gairloch Golf Club celebrated its centenary.

The fish-farming training centre at Seafield near Kishorn was reprieved by Inverness Technical College.

A bid to convert Duncraig Castle into a youth hostel was opposed by members of the local community. The castle had stood empty for nearly a decade while Highland Council sought a suitable use for it. It later went on the open market.

Infectious Salmon Anaemia affected stocks on several west-coast fish farms.

Scallop fishing was banned off the west coast when a toxic bloom which causes amnesiac shellfish poisoning was found in some scallops.

Lochcarron Shinty Club won its first senior trophy, the Balliemore Cup.

The Highland Small Communities Housing Trust was established to buy land for rural housing, and has since bought sites in Shieldaig and Gairloch.

A community group, the Isle Martin Trust, was formed in Ullapool to accept ownership of the island from the R.S.P.B.

An attempt by a local community trust to buy Fernaig Estate failed, the land being sold to a higher bidder. But the trust subsequently made a small purchase from the new owner *(see 2000)*. Elsewhere, a community trust bought Knoydart - this followed the purchase of Eigg by a local trust in 1997. The First Minister of the new Scottish Executive, Donald Dewar, introduced a Land Reform bill in 1999.

No More Kelping

A death-knell sounded in 1998 for an industry once vital to Wester Ross, gathering kelp, when Ayrshire firm Kelco ceased buying from their last remaining suppliers in the islands.

Right: Church of Scotland, Kinlochewe

Below: Shieldaig before the coastal protection scheme was built

Left: Gairloch High School, opened 1994

A Time to Reflect

With the millennium bug safely negotiated, life moved on. But as this brief survey of the year 2000 shows, many issues remained as before: the need for a pier here, the state of the roads there, worries about fishing and crofting. The fight to save a tiny church even evoked the values of a century earlier.

Diary of a Year

2000

A new pier at Ard Dubh, Applecross, was opened . The old pier at Camusterrach had been of limited use, as boats could only land at high tide. Ten prawn boats now fished from Applecross. Fuel facilities and access roads were provided, with the overall £260,000 cost being met by Ross & Cromarty Enterprise, PESCA, and Highland Council.

Plans for a new pier at Glenelg were approved. The £500,000 project included a new slipway and moorings. One local commented that "apart from the roads and a few council houses this will be the first money put into Glenelg since the Bernera Barracks in 1728."

Applecross fire station was opened. A new fire engine was also provided.

The Church of Scotland at Kinlochewe was re-opened, having closed three years earlier. The local community had raised £2,000 to restore the building, which Pat Wilson, owner of Kinlochewe Estate, had prevented from being sold by refusing to part with the land on which it stands. The community undertook to maintain it.

Torridon and Lochcarron medical practices co-operated to ensure that a nurse would always be on-call in one district and a doctor in the other.

Kishorn shop re-opened under new ownership after closing two years before.

Achmore Village Hall was re-developed at a cost of £200,000, with the local community having raised nearly £20,000. The hall was re-opened with a ceilidh in November.

The committee of Ullapool Village Hall were awarded £90,000 to restore it.

Strathcarron Station was given a new lease of life as the Strathcarron Centre for training in Information Technology and business, managed by former postmistress Kristine Mackenzie.

Applecross Historical Society made plans to set up Clachan Heritage Centre.

The Venture Trust outward-bound project at Hartfield House, Applecross, was reprieved after losing Home Office grant funding, when the Department of Employment & Education along with several other charities offered grants to allow four staff to be re-employed and rehabilitation courses to resume.

Lochcarron Shinty Club just failed to gain promotion to the National League Premier Division, when Skye defeated them in the final game and went up instead.

Plans to establish Two Lochs Radio, a radio station serving communities around Loch Gairloch and Loch Ewe, were helped by the award of funding for equipment.

A new path linked others, creating a circular walk around Flowerdale. The path up Stac Pollaidh was restored by Ross & Cromarty Footpath Trust after £30,000 was raised by public appeal.

A new development in tourism was the Food Festival. One was held in Gairloch over four days in May, another in Skye & Lochalsh over a week in September. Skye & Lochalsh Enterprise now employed a Food & Drink Development Manager to promote a sustainable food economy, encouraging crofters and producers to supply retail and catering outlets.

Local representatives on Highland Council promoted the Wester Ross 2000 initiative, assessing community needs with a view to estalishing an economic development fund.

Great Wilderness Challenge 2000

The Great Wilderness Challenge of 2000 had an entry of 538 competitors, with 145 runners and 393 walkers. The money raised for charity by the event was a record £110,000, making a total of £778,000 since 1986. The Highland Hospice continued to be the main charity supported.

The record time for the men's 25-mile run remained Jonathan Musgrave's 2 hours 48 mins 21 secs, and for women Christine Menhennet with 3 hours 21 mins 36 secs.

For details, contact Alex MacRae, 11 Mellon Charles, Aultbea, IV22 2JN. Tel. 01445 731238.

Right: Runners leave Corrie Hallie, 2000

Land and Conservation

Fernaig Community Trust bought over 100 acres of agricultural land from the new proprietor of Fernaig Estate, John Denham, assisted by a grant from the Community Land Unit of Highlands & Islands Enterprise.

The Scottish Land Fund was set up to offer grants to communities wishing to buy and regenerate land. The fund's main office was located in Lochalsh.

Various proposals made by Scottish Natural Heritage (SNH) in 2000 included designating ten lochs between Poolewe and Kinlochewe as Sites of Special Scientific Interest (SSSI). Two other lochs in the area were already in that category. SNH also designated Rassal Ashwood, Kishorn, which was already an SSSI, as a Special Area of Conservation. The moves were seen by some local residents as excessive red tape. Plans by Assynt Crofters Trust for a hydro-electric project had recently met with objections from SNH because of the likely impact on rare breeding birds.

The Cuillins were controversially offered for sale for £10 million.

Fish-Farming

A public meeting at Aultbea discussed Marine Harvest McConnell's application to increase the tonnage of salmon (or biomass) which they were permitted to produce at their Aultbea and Naast farm sites in Loch Ewe, while also introducing new sea-lice treatments.

Over 50 objections were received by the Scottish Environmental Protection Agency (SEPA). SEPA subsequently refused Marine Harvest an increase in permitted biomass, both at Loch Ewe and at another site in Loch Torridon. Indeed, SEPA went further and actually cut the tonnage permitted at Loch Ewe from 2002, commenting that the impact of fish-farming on aquatic life in the loch was presently unacceptable. Marine Harvest reduced staff at Loch Ewe from 16 to 8.

* * *

During 2000, Nutreco, owners of Marine Harvest, bought Hydro Seafoods. The firm now employed 4,900 people worldwide, including 1,000 in Scotland.

* * *

Another public meeting in the autumn discusssed an application by Ardessie Salmon for a big increase in permitted biomass at their sites in Little Loch Broom.

* * *

Smolt-producers Kinloch Damph Ltd, based near Kishorn and employing 40 people, signed a deal with an Icelandic firm to import eggs from that country.

Plane Crashes

A light aircraft flying from Inverness to Benbecula crashed into the north-facing cliffs of Liathach in Torridon in December, killing the pilot and his passenger. Despite a widespread search, it was not until many months later that the plane's wreckage was discovered by chance.

Castaways

Of various programmes depicting life in the Highlands and Islands, the most discussed was *Castaway*, which featured a group living on the island of Taransay off Harris for a year. There were comments that filming the life of a 'real' island community such as Tanera Mor would have been more instructive.

A ScotRail train heads west from Balnacra to Kyle

New Hydro Scheme

First for 30 Years

A new hydro-electric scheme was authorised on the Abhainn Cuileig river south of Corrieshalloch Gorge. It was the first scheme built by Hydro-Electric (as the North of Scotland Hydro-Electric Board was now known) for 30 years. In response to concerns about the local environment, the company agreed that the power station and 2.5km pipeline would be located underground. The construction project promised 40 jobs at its peak, at a projected cost of £3m. The scheme would supply 3 megawatts of power.

Hydro-Electric was now part of Scottish & Southern Energy, and its 56 hydro-electric power stations were centrally controlled by computer.

The Abhainn Cuileig scheme was one of a number proposed in line with the Scottish Renewables Obligation, which stipulated that 10% of all power was to be obtained from renewable sources by 2010. The Scottish Executive promised to subsidise each unit of electricity thus produced.

A 240kw hydro-electric scheme was opened in Assynt in a joint venture between Assynt Crofters Trust and Highland Light & Power Ltd, Dundee.

Controversial Experiment

A trial planting of genetically modified crops at Munlochy on the Black Isle was authorised during 2000.

Water Water Everywhere

Water supplies in a number of communities were disrupted by problems with ageing pipes.

The sometimes doubtful nature of 20th century 'progress' is illustrated in a controversy over the Highlands' most abundant resource, water.

Now on tap in nearly all homes in Wester Ross, water was routinely treated with chemicals such as chlorine to 'improve' it under requirements of European laws. As a result the finest water in Britain was sometimes rendered undrinkable. The level of chlorination so angered one resident in **Applecross** that he refused to pay his water charges in protest. The North of Scotland Water Authority subsequently built a filtration and water treatment plant in the area.

2000 (continued)

Project Honours Gavin Maxwell's Memory

In May 2000, the recently formed Eilean Ban Trust opened the Bright Water Centre at Kyleakin, and began operating boat-trips from the village to Eilean Ban, the 'white island', in the shadow of the Skye Bridge. The island is famous through its connection with Gavin Maxwell in the late 1960s, and John Lister-Kaye's book *The White Island*. It had been leased to the Trust (whose members are from Kyle and Kyleakin) for £1 a year by the Scottish Office, who had bought it prior to construction of the Skye Bridge.

Closed-circuit cameras relay pictures from the island to screens in the Bright Water Centre. The project was backed by the Born Free Foundation, supported by actress Virginia Mckenna, star of the film *Ring of Bright Water*.

Forestry

The biggest crofter forestry scheme to be launched in Wester Ross involved nine townships and 3000 acres of land owned by the Applecross Estate. Funding of over £2m was awarded by the Forestry Commission, with £100,000 from the Millennium Forest for Scotland Trust. Crofters were promised £670,000 over a 15-year period from the Farm Woodland Premium Scheme, to be used on township improvements, though a Fearnbeg crofter questioned this assertion.

Among other crofter forestry schemes set up was one at Achintee near Strathcarron, where 140 hectares of native woodland were planted.

Gaelic News

No More News

In December the daily Gaelic news bulletin *Telefios* ceased broadcasting. Meanwhile there was concern that television companies, worried by low audience figures, were broadcasting Gaelic television programmes too late at night.

In a new Education Bill, the Scottish Executive formally acknowledged the need for primary schools to provide Gaelic-medium education.

Iomairt Chaluim Chille - the 'Columba Initiative' - was launched to encourage links between the Gaelic communities of Scotland and Ireland.

The *Columba 1400 Centre*, named in commemoration of the 1400th anniversary of the death of St Columba, opened at Staffin on Skye.

Progress in Education

The new Ullapool High School was officially opened in April by Scottish Education Minister Sam Galbraith. The building included a community wing with a theatre, library, meeting-rooms and computer facilities. 210 pupils currently attended the school, taught by 26 teachers.

Progress in establishing a University of the Highlands and Islands continued, with courses leading to recognised degrees now offered at 13 further education colleges throughout the Highlands, from Shetland in the north to Perth in the south, and including the Gaelic college on Skye.

A new Centre of Excellence for Traditional Music was established at Plockton High School. Funded by Highland Council and the Scottish Executive, the Centre offered residential places to promising young musicians, under a Director reporting to the Rector of Plockton High School.

Roads and Transport

During 2000, the Scottish Executive invited bids from parties interested in taking over the management of the trunk-road network in the North of Scotland. A bid from existing contractor Highland Council was rejected in favour of the private consortium BEAR Scotland Ltd, whose contract became effective from April 2001.

There was concern over high petrol prices. One survey noted that motorists living in rural areas of the Highlands paid up to £7.50 more per tank of petrol than those living in cities.

Challenges to the legality of toll payments on the Skye Bridge continued.

The Highlands and Islands Public Transport Forum was launched. The need for a Highlands Transport Authority to co-ordinate all transport services was advocated, but interested parrties agreed this was a long way off.

The European Commission held an inquiry into the legality of the annual subsidy given by the government to Caledonian MacBrayne Ltd to operate west coast ferries. It was agreed that the subsidy did not break rules by distorting the market.

Western Isles Council continued to oppose Sunday sailings between Stornoway and Ullapool.

Fishing News

There seemed no end in prospect to a dispute over the damage done to the sea-bed by trawlers in lochs between Loch Torridon and Loch Hourn. These lochs were already closed to trawling for six months of the year, but creelmen continued to press for a complete ban, as in Loch Gairloch. John Home Robertson, Deputy Minister for Rural Affairs at the Scottish Executive, visited Torridon to learn more about the issues, attending a meeting at Shieldaig. Afterwards he called for further research to be carried out by Stirlng University - to the anger of creel fishermen who argued enough studies had been done.

Highland Council applied for a new Regulating Order under which a local committee would take responsibility for managing all shellfish stocks, with the exception of prawns, round the Highland coastline.

Scallop fishermen in Lochalsh protested to the Ministry of Defence that Royal Navy divers had been helping themselves to scallops from the sea-bed in the Inner Sound while working for BUTEC.

Gairloch Harbour Users' Group complained about a lack of investment by Highland Council. Two fish-processing businesses had closed in recent years: Gairloch Seafoods Ltd and Amazon Seafood (UK) Ltd.

Right: Ullapool High School

Below: Kyle, with the Skye bridge in background

Left: The Kyle-Kyleakin ferry, with the Skye bridge under construction in 1994

A Century of Entertainment

FOR A SMALL and scattered population, the people of Wester Ross have always managed to enjoy a wide range of entertainments and social activity.

Concerts, amateur dramatics, Highland games, shinty, society meetings - rarely a day went by (apart from Sundays) without a social or sporting event in some district. Where facilities were lacking, local people often worked together to provide them.

Gaelic Singing and Ceilidhs

In the first decades of the 20th century, when everybody spoke Gaelic, a knowledge of songs in the language came as second nature. Ceilidhs and other social get-togethers would, as often as not, include impromptu Gaelic singing and story-telling. Everyone knew the best local singers. There were Gaelic choirs in Lochalsh and Poolewe.

John S.Mackenzie from Achterneed was a regular visitor between the wars, showing slides on his magic lantern while singing Gaelic songs associated with places illustrated. The South-West Ross and Wester Ross Provincial Mods have been popular annual events for many years.

As the century passed, a generation of children grew up without being taught the language by their parents, and inevitably, Gaelic culture went into decline. Recently, however, there has been a remarkable revival of interest in all types of traditional music and Gaelic singing. This has been helped by the schools and the *Feis* movement; *Feis Rois* have organised residential tuition courses for primary children since 1986 and secondary children since 1990 (for adults too since 1991).

One tradition which has gradually been fading away in the second half of the 20th century is the ceilidh itself. Those informal evenings of story-telling and song are almost a thing of the past. Television and video have taken much of the blame.

Piping and Dancing

Wester Ross has a long tradition of piping, in the past through parents passing skills down to their children. The South-West Ross Piping Society and Conchra Pipes & Drums helped stimulate interest there from the 1960s, and from 1973 Norman Gillies and Iain MacFadyen taught piping to school pupils throughout the area. In 1977 Willie Macrae and others formed the Ullapool & District Junior Pipes & Drums, still thriving today.

Highland dancing is as popular as ever, and latterly teams of young dancers from Lochcarron and Ullapool have given the public much enjoyment.

Magic Lantern, Film and Theatre

Long before the first cinemas came to the Highlands at the time of the Great War, magic lantern shows were popular attractions, put on by touring entertainers or 'cinematographists', and also given at many lairds' Christmas parties.

In mid-century, regular film-shows were put on by the Highlands and Islands Film Guild and recently this role has been taken on by the Screen Machine mobile cinema, which makes regular visits with the latest releases.The nearest full-time cinema is in Inverness. Dingwall Picture House closed in 1980.

Amateur dramatics also flourished in Wester Ross throughout the 20th century, but particularly in earlier years. Evenings of one-act plays or humorous sketches were popular. South-West Ross has a long tradition of annual drama festivals. The nearest professional theatre venue is Eden Court, Inverness, opened in 1976.

Games, Galas & Guilds

Highlights in the social and sporting calendar are the Highland Games, including the Coigach Gathering in June, Lochcarron Games (the area's biggest event) and Applecross Games in July. Much work goes into organising these events. In former days other places, including Gairloch, also held games. Kyle has a Gala Week, and sheepdog trials and crofters' shows are traditional fixtures.

The Women's Guild and SWRI have long flourished in Wester Ross. So have several Field Clubs and Heritage Societies, some of which run local museums.Whist drives were formerly very popular, usually to raise funds for good causes.

Sport and the Great Outdoors

Two senior shinty clubs, Lochcarron and Kinlochshiel, were active in Wester Ross at the end of the century. Kinlochshiel was formed by merging three older clubs. Communities like Kinlochewe and Lochbroom previously fielded teams.

Football is as popular as ever. Most clubs have survived ups and down as player resources or finances have varied. Some, like Gairloch and Aultbea, have merged. Skye and Lochalsh Rugby Club travel widely to find opposition.

Four golf clubs were open in 2000, Gairloch having survived since the 1890s and Lochcarron since 1908. Great commitment is required from a relatively small number of members, but recently Gairloch opened a clubhouse cafe, and Lochcarron members have bought their land and built a machinery shed. Fishing and sailing remain ever-popular. Several districts had shooting clubs in earlier years; Achnasheen still does. Four mountain rescue teams give their time to assist those who venture into the hills and come to grief, while many others assist or participate in the Great Wilderness Challenge. Indoors, badminton enjoys a special popularity in South-West Ross. Three swimming-pools and three leisure centres provide excellent sports facilities.

Venues and Promoters

The main venue for dances, plays, concerts, film shows or talks was always the village hall or drill hall. In the days before radio and television, the value to a community of its hall as a meeting-place and hub of social life went without saying.

Concerts and plays were also put on in local schools, especially in more remote communities where there was no hall. Pupils' concerts and plays often brought a community together.

Hotels and pubs also play their part in hosting live music. The Ceilidh Place in Ullapool even opened a special arts venue, the clubhouse, in the late 1970s. In recent years, community centres have been built in several villages. The new High Schools at Gairloch and Ullapool each have a community wing including a theatre.

In the last thirty years, promoters such as West Coast Arts in the Gairloch area, and *Feis Rois* serving the whole county, have arranged events and brought many performers to Wester Ross.

Military

In the early years of the century, there was a darker purpose to some leisure activity. Men in every district gave up a substantial part of their free time to serve in Volunteer Companies, re-named the Territorial Army in 1908. Weekly drill meetings were held and annual camps attended. One incidental benefit of the Volunteer era was the building of a number of Drill Halls, some still in use today for social purposes. Aultbea's Village Hall is another legacy of military activity, in the Second World War. The Territorial Army is still active in Ross-shire, as are several wings of the Air Training Corps.

Who Did What in 2000

Those making a living from fishing made up a much smaller proportion of the workforce in 2000 than in earlier times. However, there were new jobs in related industries, like fish-processing at Kyle and Gairloch. Shellfish was the main local catch, much going for export, even from remote districts, thanks to visiting buyers such as MBBS Ltd.

Fish-farming was a major employer, undreamt-of in 1900. Tourism was now vital to the economy, many hotels, pubs, and restaurants providing livelihoods. Cruise operators, craftshops and other visitor attractions also catered for visitors. The retail sector included supermarkets.

Various organisations at the BUTEC base in Kyle employed over 100 people. Many staff worked for Hydro-Electric, NOSWA, British Telecom and Forest Enterprise, for haulage contractors and transport operators such as Westerbus, and for construction and civil engineering firms.

Private estates still employed men outdoors, though jobs in domestic service were now rare. Several quarries were open. Various departments of the Highland Council employed staff in schools, libraries, service points, leisure centres and on the roads. There were five medical and two dental practices and five residential care homes. Self-employment was important, now featuring internet and telecommunications firms, and B&B and self-catering establishments, as well as traditional skills. Crofting continued to be a source of income for many people.

A Century of Crofting

There are currently 72 crofting townships in Wester Ross and South West Ross. Though few crofters now work the land or keep cattle, most have sheep, and crofting is still seen as a way of life worth supporting.

When the 20th century began, almost everyone in Wester Ross depended on crofting to survive. By its end, only a few did. This might seem, at first glance, a record of decline, but the truth is more complex.

Crofters are, on the whole, better off than a century ago; and while much of their income is earned by other means, crofting was never intended to provide a full-time living. By the end of the century the debate about its future was as much about preserving a way of life as ensuring crofters could live.

The century saw many changes, with long years of struggle, changes in the law and occasional tensions between crofters, Government and those in crofting administration.

Until 1912 responsibility for day-to-day administration, including rent levels, lay with the *Crofters Commission*, set up under the original Crofters Act of 1886, while the *Congested Districts Board* had been set up in 1897 to provide grants to improve land, build roads and, if possible, buy back estates lost to crofting during the clearances - unfortunately only one or two were purchased and none here. In 1912 the Congested Districts Board was replaced by the *Board of Agriculture*, while the duties of the Crofters Commission were divided between the Board of Agriculture and *Scottish Land Court*. The Board of Agriculture introduced a useful source of funding for crofters, the *Crofter House Scheme*, under which loans were made available, and 4,000 houses were built by 1939.

Early in the century, crofters were required to live permanently on their croft holdings. However, a legal case in 1917 led to a relaxation of this rule, with the result that by mid-century many crofters lived and worked elsewhere, keeping their croft-house as a second home. This led to a sharp decline in the amount of land worked.

Under the *Land Settlement (Scotland) Act, 1919,* the Board of Agriculture was given powers to purchase land for ex-servicemen as smallholdings or stock clubs. Unfortunately little was achieved by the time the Department of Agriculture & Fisheries for Scotland (DAFS) replaced the Board of Agriculture in 1920.

W.MacKintosh

Depopulation

For the Edinburgh-based authorities, the main concern in the crofting counties between the wars was depopulation. The *Crofter Counties Roads* scheme was introduced to assist County Councils to improve the roads infrastructure. But by the mid-1930s the Government was so concerned about Highland depopulation that it set up a Commission to find ways to encourage investment. Unfortunately the war stalled any hopes of progress.

After the war, farm prices were guaranteed, and the *Hill Farming Act 1946* offered grants to those on marginal land or 'less favoured areas', for the re-seeding of hill pastures, building of cattle shelters and so on. Unfortunately many crofters did not qualify for grants as their crofts were too small. However, the *Crofter Building Grants and Loan Scheme* was an important innovation which offered assistance on favourable terms to crofters wishing to build or repair their house or to undertake construction work.

Absenteeism

The Taylor Commission

In 1952 a Commission of Enquiry was set up by the Government to examine problems in crofting. The Commission was headed by Thomas Taylor, Principal of Aberdeen University, who consulted crofting communities, landowners and other interested organisations. He identified a number of problems, notably the question of how to terminate absentee tenancies and dispose of vacant crofts, and the problem of elderly crofters neglecting their land but refusing to give it up. Other needs were identified, including easier access to livestock markets, provision of capital grants, and the compiling of a detailed register of crofts. Unfortunately the Government did not take many of Taylor's recommendations into account and the main thrust of the *Crofters Act, 1955* was more efficiency. It re-established the

Crofters Commission, based in Inverness, which assumed responsibility for most aspects of crofting, although DAFS continued to administer existing grants.

No Enforcement

The Crofters Commission got off to a shaky start. A register of crofts took five years to compile. The Commission tried but mostly failed to persuade elderly, inactive resident crofters to give up their crofts in favour of young people. Some success, however, was achieved in persuading absentees to assign their holdings to resident crofters. But efforts to encourage several townships, such as Big Sand near Gairloch, to amalgamate crofts into more effective units came to nothing.

The *Crofter Counties Agricultural Grants Scheme* was a welcome innovation, however, offering substantial grants for outhouses, drainage and fencing. Other key grants now paid included *Hill Livestock Compensatory Allowance (HLCA)* and *Sheep Annual Premium.*

In 1961 the Government introduced a Bill, after consulting the Crofters Commission, to enforce the amalgamation of small crofts into larger units, giving the most efficient crofters more land. But many crofters protested that a croft was intended to be held inalienably, with each family having the right to pass it down. Local unions were formed to co-ordinate protests. The proposed Bill was eventually amended and the *Crofters Act, 1961* introduced only minor changes.

New Board, New Union

In 1965 the Labour Government set up the Highlands & Islands Development Board to encourage new industries and create jobs, and try to halt long-term population decline in the Highlands. At first, the Board concentrated its efforts on more populous areas, for example helping to fund an aluminium smelter at Invergordon. Crofting areas were initially viewed as purely agricultural.

The main development in crofting in the 1970s was the *Crofters Reform Act* of 1976 *(see above)*. In 1984 the Scottish Crofters' Union was established, enabling crofters to be consulted by Government about issues of the day, at the same time offering members legal and insurance services.

In 1991 Highlands & Islands Enterprise (successor to the HIDB) launched the *Rural Enterprise Programme* in Wester Ross to offer financial incentives to crofters to diversify into other business. The *Croft New Entrant Scheme* was introduced in the mid-1990s to encourage older crofters and absentees to make way for young people. The buy-out by local crofters of North Assynt in 1993 renewed a debate about the benefits of landownership, and HIE set up a Community Land Unit, which bought an estate on Skye for crofting.

Arguments about Ownership

In 1976 the *Crofters Reform Act* gave crofters the right to buy their crofts. But there was controversy over whether this would benefit crofting in the long run.

One factor behind the legislation was a longstanding injustice whereby, when croft land was sold, the landowner rather than the crofters benefited, by being paid a 'development value' for the land, while crofters received an 'agricultural value' - usually a paltry sum by comparison. Thus on Skye in 1972, eight crofters received £12 for part of the common grazings after it was sold for housing, and the laird was paid £8000. The Crofters Reform Act ensured crofters would in future be entitled to share payments of the development value.

The Act gave crofters the right to buy their croft at a price equivalent to fifteen times the annual rent. However, nothing in crofting is straightforward, and as opponents of the Act had feared, a number of crofters bought their land, de-crofted it, and then sold it on the open market - with considerable acreages lost to crofting forever. On the other hand, those who bought their croft but remained on it discovered that they were penalised by forfeiting grants payable only to crofting *tenants*. By the early 1980s, the Crofters Commission itself stated that some crofters would be ill-advised to buy their holdings. Many crofters did not bother. By 1993, just one in six crofts in Ross-shire (333 out of 1829) were owner-occupied.

Looking Back and Ahead

The decline in crofting activity in Wester Ross during the 20th century was dramatic. Back in 1900 almost everyone shared a day-to-day, year-by-year routine, looking after cattle and sheep and growing crops on their in-bye land. During the century the number of crofts in the Highlands fell from 21,000 to 17,500. The main activity was keeping sheep.

However, of those actively crofting, many continued to be successful, and the Drumbuie crofters *(see 1996)* illustrated what could be achieved. And the demand for holdings at Balmacara suggested that the crofting way of life was still valued.

On the Croft, 2000

New Crofts

The National Trust for Scotland assigned eight tenancies on what was the first crofting township to be created in the Highlands for more than fifty years, at Balmacara Square, Lochalsh.

32 hectares were transferred from Balmacara Home Farm's in-bye land to crofting tenure, and 100 hectares of hill ground converted to woodland, to be managed jointly by the NTS, crofters, and the community.

New crofts ranged from 4 to 10 acres. Derelict farm steadings were restored, and five houses and four workshops built, as well as an interpretative facility. Funding was provided by the NTS, Highland Council, Skye & Lochalsh Enterprise, SNH and Scottish Homes.

HLCA Abolished

Hill Livestock Compensatory Allowance, a subsidy which for many years had made it economic for crofters to keep sheep, was replaced by the *Less Favoured Area Support Scheme*, under which payments were linked to acreage rather than headage (i.e. the number of animals kept). Crofters objected this gave no incentive to keep animals. Some were also affected by re-assessments of land as rough grazing instead of permanent grass.

Loss of Croft Land

Plans to allow a housing association to use common grazings to build houses at Firemore, Inverasdale, upset some crofters who felt no croft land should be given up.

Crofter's Accolade

Ewen Mackinnon, Strathcarron, was voted Scottish *Crofter of the Year*. Among improvements to his croft, 5000 metres of new fencing had been put up, access tracks improved, land re-seeded or drained, bracken reduced, a flock of 400 sheep built up. Mr Mackinnon also found time to serve as the local Highland Councillor.

Lament for the Fishing-Stations

The closing years of the 20th century marked the sad demise of an old tradition: salmon-fishing with bag-nets. During the 1990s this type of fishing lingered at a few remaining fishing-stations like Badentarbet and Red Point, but when it ceased at Red Point in 2000 an era seemed to have gone for good.

Willie MacKintosh of Strath, Gairloch, is a crofter, farmer and fisherman. As well as leasing the Red Point fishing-station he used to own a fishing-boat, *Dona M,* and landed prawns, cod and other fish at Gairloch harbour. He is also the tenant of Red Point farm, and he crofts at Strath. But while the salmon season was open, Willie spent most days at the bag-netting station at Red Point, which he worked for 15 seasons from 1986.

The reason he stopped? There were simply no more wild salmon. He would re-start at a moment's notice, he says, if the fish were to return, and keeps a watchful eye on the sea when he drives to Red Point farm. Unfortunately he feels the stocks will not recover. And he has no doubt of the main cause - fish-farming.

In his first few years at Red Point, Willie made good catches and had good financial returns. Though the work was quite hard, with a lot of maintenance work to be done on nets, it was rewarding and it gave regular employment to five men full-time for about half the year, with another part-time as a driver, and his wife Mairi also selling fish and taking orders.

The salmon season is from February to September - in practice Willie would be at Red Point daily from about mid-March to August. There were many good days when hundreds of salmon were caught. The normal pattern was to put out around eight bag-nets at a time, and haul these in three or four times a day. The fish were sold either locally or at Aberdeen for the continental market.

In the late 1980s Willie noticed a big increase in the number of escaped farmed salmon he was catching - over 30% in 1989. In 1993, the number of sea trout he caught fell to almost nil - yet he had been netting several hundred each season. Then the number of salmon began to decline, from thousands each season to just a few hundred latterly. Scientists from DAFS were sent to examine the problem,but no solution was found. After three loss-making seasons Willie called it a day. By then, he had reduced the number of men working for him to just his son Donald.

Willie feels two factors are responsible. One is the uncontrolled rise in the number of seals, which eat salmon; but the main cause is the number of escaped farmed salmon, which have taken spawning beds from wild salmon, preventing them from breeding.

"Escaped farmed fish have a need to spawn - but they do not know where their place of birth is, as they were brought to farms from hatcheries by road, boat or helicopter. That's the missing link in the chain - they don't know which fresh water system they came from. So they go up the nearest rivers to spawn. There are so many that there isn't enough room for wild fish in the spawning beds. Escapees also eat young fish on which sea trout depend. There needs to be more control, with fish traceable by tagging or numbering of their feed bags - as stock farmers have to do."

Red Point salmon-fishing station

Can the wild salmon recover? Willie thinks not. Their lifespan is five to six years, and that has now elapsed with no improvement, which means native stocks have effectively died out. Meantime he keeps busy on the land at Red Point and Strath, with over 500 north country Cheviot ewes, 40 breeding cows and a small herd of Highland cattle, bred for their meat, which bring fair returns. His son Donald realised some time ago there was no future in the fishing so started up his own fencing contracting business. Willie himself still lives in hope about the fishing - but not expectation.

At the bothy in 1986: Donald Mackenzie, Opinan; Angus Bain, Sand; Murdo Mackenzie, Red Point; and Willie MacKintosh

Donald MacKintosh, Davie Catto and David Wade with a good haul in 1988

A Century On the Road

Motor-vehicles were seldom seen in Wester Ross before the First World War, though one or two hotels had cars and chauffeurs. A few motor-buses were already operating, for example on the Garve-Ullapool service.

Between the wars, numbers of vehicles slowly increased. In 1930, among the commercial vehicles advertised by the County Garage, Dingwall, were lorries and buses for £25, including a 3-ton Bedford lorry and a 14-seater Ford Charabanc (bus). A new Morris Oxford car cost £299, a Morris Minor £149 - a great deal of money. Other makes of the day included Essex, Singer, Armstrong-Siddeley, Wolseley and Dodge. Motorcycles cost from £48.

After the last war, as tractors became more common on the land, driving also became easier on the roads, and cars more affordable. In 1960, a new Morris Mini cost £500 (including purchase tax of £150). In 1970, most cars were still British-made: a Hillman Imp cost £766. Other popular makes included the Austin Mini, Vauxhall Victor, Triumph Herald, Singer Gazelle, Sunbeam Rapier and Ford Cortina. Some prices were still in guineas, though decimalisation was only one year away.

By 2000 a car was considered a necessity of life by many people in Wester Ross. Many vehicles were now imported.

Those who Served

From 1891 to 1975, Wester Ross was administered by Ross and Cromarty County Council. Matters of regional interest were delegated to District Committees serving South-West Ross, Lochcarron, Gairloch and Lochbroom. In 1900, Wester Ross had 13 out of 51 council members (including Lewis representatives).

Parish Councils, established in 1895, had a range of local functions included levying rates for education and poor relief, which paid for the management of the local poorhouse.

School Boards were responsible for schools in each parish until 1919, when a County Education Authority was elected.

In 1930, District Councils for South West Ross, Lochcarron, Gairloch and Lochbroom took over some of the duties of parish councils. The County Council took over responsibility for rates, and also took over the duties of the Education Authority. Parish Councils and School Boards were abolished.

In 1975, the structure of local government in the Highlands was re-organised again, and a two-tier administration set up. Highland Regional Council took control of matters including roads, education, water and planning, while Ross & Cromarty District Council took responsibility for housing and other affairs, except in South-West Ross, now covered by Skye and Lochalsh District Council.At the same time, councillors for Lewis achieved their goal of independence from Ross-shire with the election of the Western Isles Council *(Comhairle nan Eilean).*

Community Councils were created to represent local opinion and comment on planning issues, liaising with local Councillors.

In 1996 the single-tier Highland Council was set up. Dingwall continued as a centre of administration for Wester Ross, and Portree for South-West Ross. Specific functions were taken on in the 1990s by unelected bodies such as NOSWA (for water and sewerage) and Ross & Cromarty Enterprise (RACE), which was established in 1990 to assist business development.

On the Road: the A832 at Glen Docherty

Ross-shire Members of Parliament

1892-1911 J.G.Weir, Liberal. He died while still MP.
1911-1936 Ian Macpherson, Liberal. He resigned. He was Minister for Pensions for a time.
1936-1945 Malcolm Macdonald, National Government. Selected by Liberal Association. Was Dominion Secretary, Colonial Secretary, Minister of Health, and latterly British High Commissioner in Canada while still Ross-shire MP. Not re-selected by Liberals in 1945.
1945-1964 Captain John MacLeod, National Liberal. Latterly endorsed by the Unionist party and opposed by Liberals.
1964-1970 Alasdair Mackenzie, Liberal. He defeated MacLeod.
1970-1983 Hamish Gray, Conservative. He defeated Mackenzie.
1983-2000 Charles Kennedy, S.D.P. then Liberal Democrat. Current constituency is Ross, Skye and Inverness West.

Voting: At the 1900 election, just over 5,000 votes were cast. Mr Weir (Liberal) polled 3,554 votes, his Unionist opponent 1,651. At the 1997 election, 39,000 votes were cast. Liberal Democrats polled 15,472 votes, Labour 11,453, SNP 7,821, and Conservatives 4,368.

Following the establishment of the Scottish Parliament in 1999, Wester Ross gained a new level of representation. John Farquhar Munro (Liberal), a former Regional Councillor, was elected as local Member of the Scottish Parliament. In addition, several "list" MSPs, such as Maureen Macmillan (Labour), were selected by proportional representation to serve the Highlands including Wester Ross.

How Times Have Changed

Advertisements in the *Ross-shire Journal* in past years offer a reminder of how sales techniques evolved.

(1900) ***Old False Teeth Bought***. Many ladies and gentlemen have old or disused false teeth which might as well be turned into money. Messrs Fraser, Princes Street, Ipswich, buy old false teeth. If you send your teeth to them they will remit you by return of post the utmost value; or, if preferred, they will make you the best offer and hold the teeth over for your reply.

(1910) ***Dr Williams' Pink Pills***. At thirty a woman should be in the prime of charm and beauty, yet many women begin to fade before then. Wrinkles appear; dark rings surround the eyes; headaches follow, with backaches and low spirits. Dr Williams' pink pills for pale people supply the rich red blood that repairs waste, dispels disease and restores the brightness and charm of womanly health. *(Another version was aimed at men!)*

(1920) ***Otter Skins***. Wanted, good Scotch skins in any quantity. Highest prices paid, cash per return. C.W.Slater & Co Ltd, 113 Great Western Road, Glasgow.

Those who Owned the Land

Throughout the 20th century, Wester Ross continued to be owned by a small number of lairds, though a number of estates were broken up. Nearly every estate comprised extensive deer-forest, one or two sheep-farms, and crofting townships. Some proprietors, like the Gairloch Mackenzies, had - and still have - close links with the communities who live on their land. Others were sporting proprietors, interested only in the shooting and fishing rights on their land.

All estates gave considerable employment, but less so as the years passed. Some lairds were very sympathetic to the local community, especially the few who lived here permanently or for much of the year and were able to get to know their tenants' concerns and interests. Some were held in high regard by local people; others less so or not at all. When lairds were absent, their factors acted for them, with varying degrees of popularity.

In earlier years many lairds served on the county council and parish councils; this is much less the case now.

Landowners in 1900

The main lairds at the start of the century were the Duke of Sutherland (Drumrunie/Glencanisp), the Countess of Cromartie (Coigach/Inverpolly), F.Pirie (Leckmelm), Sir John Fowler (Braemore/Inverbroom), Hugh Mackenzie of Ardross (Dundonnell), Mrs Bankes (Ardlair/Letterewe), Osgood Mackenzie (Inverewe/Tournaig), Lord Mackenzie (Inveran), Sir Kenneth Mackenzie (Gairloch), Arthur Bignold (Lochrosque), Duncan Darroch (Torridon), Lord Wimborne (Glencarron/ Achnashellach), Lord Middleton (Applecross), Charles Murray (Lochcarron), Sir W.Dalgleish (Coulin), Sir Kenneth Matheson (Attadale/Lochalsh/Inverinate) and Baillie of Dochfour (Glenshiel).

Main Landowners in 1996

Owner / Principal Interest*	Estate	Acreage
	Over 20,000 acres	
P. van Vlissingen*	*Letterewe*	81,000
Sheik Mohammed*	*Killilan etc*	63,000
F.Wills*	*Applecross*	62,000
J.Mackenzie	*Gairloch (& Conon)*	56,900
National Trust for Scotland	*Kintail, Lochalsh, Torridon*	41,000
Dickinson Trust	*Strathvaich / Strathrannoch*	37,000
Roger Brothers	*Dundonnell*	33,600
E.Macpherson	*Attadale*	32,000
P.Wilson	*Kinlochewe / Lochrosque*	30,000
I.Melville*	*Kinlochluichart*	27,400
H.van Beuningen*	*Inverlael / Foich*	23,600
	12,500 - 20,000 acres	
E.Robson	*Inverbroom*	19,000
J.Macdonald-Buchanan	*Inveran*	18,500
P.Smith	*Coulin*	18,300
Lord Burton*	*Glenshiel / Cluanie (part)*	17,000
M.Pattinson	*Couldoran*	16,900
Execs. for Mrs M.Dunphie	*Eilean Darach*	16,500
A.Fenwick	*Langwell*	15,800
E.Vestey*	*Drumrunie & Glencanisp*	15,800
E.Scobie	*Rhidorroch*	15,100
A.Sladen	*Glencarron*	15,000
J.Hardy*	*Aultbea*	15,000
T.Gray, D.Carr-Smith*	*Ben Damph*	14,820
T.Wills	*Achnashellach*	14,800
Mrs A.Maclay*	*Gruinard*	14,800
Scottish Wildlife Trust	*Ben More Coigach, I.Ristol*	14,600
C.Stroyan	*West Monar / Pait*	13,500
J.Ruggles-Brise	*Ledgowan*	13,300
D.Davies*	*Inverpolly*	12,500

(Source: Who Owns Scotland *by A.Wightman, pub. by Canongate)*

Summaries of Change

1900-1950

The main change was the sale by the Mathesons of much of their land. In the 1920s the Forestry Commission began to buy land, in the 1940s the National Trust for Scotland also.

Ardlair ca.1905 Sold by Bankes family to Marquis of Zetland
Achnashellach Sold by 1910 by Lord Wimborne to Mr Bainbridge
Attadale Sold in 1910 by Sir K.J.Matheson to tenant Mr Schroder
Torridon Sold c.1910 on death of Mr Darroch to Mr MacDonald-Buchanan. Sold 1924 to Sir Charles Gordon, who sub-divided Wester Alligin (retained by him) & Torridon (sold to Mr Gunter).
Inverinate Sold by Sir K.J.Matheson to Sir K.A Fraser c.1910
Leckmelm Sold c1912 by Mr Pirie to Major Fraser
Ullapool Sold by Duncan Matheson in 1918
Lochalsh (west) Sold 1918 by Sir K.J.Matheson to Sir D.Hamilton
Kinlochewe (60,000 acres) Sold in 1920 to Mr E.Hickman after being separated from Gairloch Estate
Rhidorroch Sold in 1920 by Countess of Cromartie to Mr Rose
Lochrosque Sold in 1920 by Lady Bignold to Mr Hanbury
Braemore Sold in 1920 by Sir Montague Fowler
Applecross Sold in 1929 by Lord Middleton to the Wills family
Dundonnell Sub-divided by Maitlands to form **Eilean Darach Estate.** The rest sold as Dundonnell to Sir Michael Peto
Lochalsh Left by Lady Hamilton in 1944 to National Trust for Scotland
Kintail Sold in 1944 to the National Trust for Scotland
Attadale Sold in 1945 to Col.M.Gibbs
Lochcarron Sold in 1945 by Mr Murray to Mr Greg
Aultbea Sold to Mr MacLean

1951-2000

A number of estates were acquired by limited companies or transferred to family trusts. Several estates were bought by Dutch and Scandinavian interests.

Attadale Sold in 1952 to Mr I.Macpherson (now owned by his son)
Letterewe Sold 1950s to Col. Whitbread (his son later sold the land)
Inverewe Gifted in 1952 to the National Trust for Scotland
Rhidorroch Sold to Major I.Mackay Scobie
Dundonnell Sold in 1954 by Sir Michael Peto to the Roger brothers
Inverlael Sold in 1959 to Mr Whitteridge
Leckmelm Sold to Mr Beattie
Inverpolly Sold in 1960 by Earl of Cromartie to Mr Davies
Inverbroom Sold in 1960 on death of Sir M.Fowler to Mr L.Robson
Torridon Sold in 1960 to Earl of Lovelace, on whose death in 1967 it went to National Trust for Scotland in lieu of death duties
Ben Damph Sold in early 1960s by Earl of Lovelace
Wester Alligin Gifted by Gordons to National Trust for Scotland
Foich (then part of Braemore) Sold to Mr J.H.Dewhurst
Fannich Sold in 1976 by Mr Sandeman to Dutch company
Foich Sold in 1976 by J.Dewhurst to Mr van Beuningen
Letterewe/Ardlair (21,000 acres) Sold 1978 to Paul van Vlissingen
Kinlochewe *(part)* Sold in 1993 to Paul van Vlissingen
Lochrosque and **Kinlochewe** *(part)* Sold 1993 to Mr Pat Wilson
Coulin Sold in 1996 to Capt. P.Smith
Dundonnell Bequeathed by Roger brothers in 1998 to manservant on whose behalf the estate was then sold to Sir Tim Rice
Runie Sold to Mr D.Bulmer of neighbouring **Keanchulish**

Old Ways, New Ways

Many people believe there are fewer "characters" around these days. That may go hand in hand with a loss of old customs and crafts. Gone are the blacksmiths, millers, whisky-distillers, boat-builders, salmon-netters (along with the salmon), and tinkers. The tinkers like Essie Stewart and her family brought colour to life, with their horses and carts and tinsmiths' skills. At least, late in the day, scholars like Hamish Henderson realised what a lore of Gaelic songs they knew, and had the foresight to record them.

Old ways of doing things are missed, too. The steamers which plied the coast were not just lifelines, they brought life to every community along the way. Roy Macintyre wrote of visits to Gairloch pier in his youth during the war. "Excursions to see the herring boats discharging their catches or the MacBrayne's steamer discharging goods for the shops, and coal puffers being unloaded, were always full of interest." Times change, people with them; but the old ways are always worth keeping in mind.

New Year

Well into the 20th century, New Year celebrations lasted for days, and the 'Old' New Year on 13th January was widely observed. New Year's Day used to be marked by several sporting encounters. In Lochcarron, Jeantown played Slumbay at shinty, and in Plockton, as Tom MacIver recalled, there was a shinty match on the foreshore between local 'uppies' and 'downies'.

"There were no goalposts, and as far as I can recollect a score was registered when the ball was driven into Ob an Duine at one end or past a mark on the shore at Dall at the other end. There did not appear to be a time limit on the game, which was probably terminated either by the incoming tide or, more likely, the need of rival teams to partake of New Year refreshments."

Uppies and Downies

Plockton also staged a summer football match between teams from 'Up the Street' and 'Down the Street', as recalled in an article of the late 1930s contributed by Charles M.MacRae. 'The street' was Harbour Street: the 'ups' lived at the Ob an Duine end or on Cooper Street, while the downs were from Innes Street, Bank Street, and that end. The author was clearly an 'uppie'!

"Though Innes St might try to look down on the others and boast that it held all that was great in the village, still even the elite of Innes St spoke of Harbour St as 'the street'. The street was quite willing to allow Innes St to have all three churches, manses, the school and Inland Revenue office. But the folks on the street preferred their glorious outlook up Loch Carron..."

Goodbye Gaelic

During the 20th century many old ways of life disappeared, some slowly, some almost overnight. Included in that list, sadly, must be Gaelic - no longer the everyday language of the home.

K.C.Mackenzie of Poolewe recalls that when he was at school in the 1930s "Gaelic was even then fairly rapidly losing its struggle for survival".

His parents, like many, used English when talking to their children, in the belief that this would improve their educational prospects. They had been persuaded to "protect" their children from Gaelic. Mr Mackenzie and others have at least helped to preserve local Gaelic usages with booklets like his *Place Names in and around Poolewe*, one of several similar publications in recent years.

Sunday

In the late 20th century there was a sharp decline in observance of the Sabbath. Many people still respect it, but some shops have begun to open and household chores are routinely done - a far cry from the time when the only activity allowed on Sunday, apart from worship and Bible study, was to tend the animals. "Even the dog knew his duties were not required," as one lady put it. Sunday retains a special feeling, however, as the lack of public transport serves to remind us (and puzzle visitors).

Tired but happy competitors complete the Great Wilderness Challenge

In with the New

It may perhaps be true that there are fewer characters in Wester Ross than there used to be, but as a new century began it was still the people and communities of this area which made it such a special place, including the many tireless voluntary helpers and local committees whose efforts keep halls or playgroups going, or the supporters of Blythswood Care, or those who take part in the Great Wilderness Challenge.

What is the 21st century likely to bring? Perhaps the only certainty is that Wester Ross will remain the finest landscape in Britain. As to the prospects for those who live here, those are ever unpredictable. This area has never been, and is never likely to be, one of the most prosperous in the country.

But while there may be material disadvantages to living here, most people will no doubt continue to make light of them and reflect, as this publication has done, that however challenging life may be, for previous generations it was harder still.